Ultimate Guide
To
Teen Life

The
Ultimate Guide
To
Teen Life

By
Yahya Bakkar

The Ultimate Guide to
Teen Life

Praise for
The Ultimate Guide to Teen Life

"Hands down, this is a MUST-READ for any teen who wants to make a positive impact in the world!"

-Rich German,
Founder of *The Gen WHY Project*

"Yahya's advice for teens is as good as it gets. I have no doubt that the wisdom in this book will inspire, influence and impact teens for years to come."

-Brooks Gibbs,
Author of *Love Is Greater Than Hate*

'I've been working as a motivator of teens for over 10 years and this book is hands down the best guide to support teen success that I've ever come across. If you are a teenager or have a teenager you care about, get this book ASAP. You won't regret it!'

-Kara Zakrzewski,
World-Class Athlete and Author

"Wow! As a rocket scientist, I was not expecting to be blown away with this book. For what it's worth, I recommend that you follow Yahya's guide to have a fun, fulfilling, and fruitful life as a teen - you will be so glad you did."

-Kantis Simmons,
Academic Success Expert & Author of
*Playing Your 'A' Game: Stay Motivated,
Remain Focused and Succeed in School
& Life*

This book is dedicated to all of the amazing teenagers out there who are looking for meaning in their lives, who are finding their voice in today's world and who want to be seen and heard for who they truly are. I don't care how bad, dumb, fat, ugly, weird, obnoxious or different other people think you are. In my eyes, you are the hope for our future.

Thank you for being alive today. I unconditionally appreciate your trust and support.

Contents

How To Avoid Boredom While Reading

In each chapter of this book, we'll discuss one common area in your life. The chapters are all about different topics, but they connect to each other, and they're in order for a reason (you need to understand the stuff at the beginning in order to understand the stuff at the end). Therefore, the first time you read this book, don't skip around. Feel free to read it at a pace you're comfortable with—this isn't a race. Then later, when there's a particular area of your life that needs some improvement, you can go back and reread a chapter that really speaks to you.

Each chapter contains challenges, in which I ask you to stop reading and think about or do something. At the end of the chapter are several discussion questions that will push you and challenge you. For you to get the best benefits from this book, you really should answer the questions. Look, no one's grading your work, and no one's giving you a sticker if you answer everything. For most of the questions, there isn't even a right or wrong answer. The only test is your life, and let me share a little secret: 90% of people who want something in their lives are unwilling to work for it. People say they want to be happier, healthier or be with their dream guy or girl, but then they do nothing and complain when it stays the same. If you have aspects of your life you want to improve and you're reading this book, you may have to put in a little bit of work. But that work can transform your life.

Inside this book, underline stuff. Highlight. Write yourself notes. Dog-ear pages that you like. It's your life, and your book, so go ahead and do what you've got to do.

Make a "My Guide to Life" journal. Answer the questions in there, copy down quotes, cut out images from a magazine that you like and add your own thoughts and opinions about what you read. Don't want a "journal?" Call it your "playbook," because each chapter is like one play that you will have to run in your life.

Sharing the book is also a great way to learn the material. Lend it to your friends. Carry it around with you. Form a discussion group so you can bounce ideas off one another. If I haven't spoken at your school or conference yet, find out who is in charge of bringing motivational speakers in and tell them to visit www.NationalYouthSpeaker.com. If you want to know why many students across America call me "The Beat-box Ninja" visit www.ShutYourMouse.com. If something in the book really spoke to you or helped you see something differently, please share it at www.YoYahya.com or email me at Yahya@YahyaBakkar.com.

All right. Enough warm-ups. Let's get this thing started. Are you ready to create an awesome life?

Introduction

Life has its easy times and its hard times. Which of these do you think are the hardest?

Is it being a baby, when the world is new and you're doing everything for the first time?

Is it being a child, adjusting to school and responsibility?

Is it when you're in college, away from home for the first time?

Is it when you get married? Buy your first house? Have children? Grow old? When is it?

I'd say it's got to be your teenage years. They're the hardest, but they can also be the best years of your life!

Everything is changing. Your body is changing, your brain is changing and your friends and family are changing. Things that were certain for the first couple years of your life are suddenly in doubt. You have to make some of the biggest decisions of your life. Rarely will you face so much change in so little time.

With all these changes, we can sometimes get so caught up in what is right in front of us that we can't see further on down the road. The adult generation that is in charge today won't be in charge forever. The problems of tomorrow will be solved by the leaders of tomorrow—and by leaders I mean you. You are a massive, untapped source of inspiration and creativity. You have the ability to adapt to any challenging situation in your life and turn it into an opportunity. In order for the world to have an amazing future, you first need to create an amazing life for yourself.

I hope this book can be your guide toward doing that.

Look, I'm not some superhero who never makes mistakes. Believe me, I've made my share of mistakes! But I've learned from them, and I hope you can learn from yours as much as I have. Maybe you can find some of the answers you're looking for. You definitely won't find all of them in this book, but I'm confident you can get *something* positive out of what you read.

You also won't find me telling you what to do or how to act. You've got enough people doing that in your life. I'm going to share some of my experiences and what I've learned from them. In the end, it's your own life, your own future and your own choice whether you take what I say to heart or not.

Here's what you will find in this book:

- **The Common Areas of Life**
  We're talking about the stuff that is part of everyone's life: fun, food, family, friends, fitness, freedom, fear, fighting, and more. You know, the stuff everyone goes through.

- **Self-Discovery**
  Sorry, this isn't a book you can breeze through and be done with. (Well, you can, but then what's the point?) This book requires you to think and reflect on who you are so you can create a positive ripple effect around you.

- **Challenging Questions that Hit Close to Home**
  Some of the questions I ask are difficult, and may even be personal. I may discuss topics that make you uncomfortable. The world isn't always pretty or pleasant, and neither are the choices we make.

Relax. This will be fun and worth your time. I promise.

- **Discussion Questions and Actions**

  This book requires your participation. Reading the words won't be enough. As we go through the chapters, I'm going to ask you some questions and challenge you to incorporate the ideas in the chapter into your life. I hope you take me up on that invitation.

- **Laugh**

  This book is not supposed to be a drag. I like to keep things light and loose. So take a deep breath and smile. This is going to be a blast!

Whether you're an honor roll student or a dropout, whether you are popular or a loner, whether you're an athlete or out of shape, whether you have a supportive family or a dysfunctional one, whether you've made good choices or poor ones, I truly believe you are an amazing person—even if other people don't believe it, or even if you don't believe it yourself. Right now, you have the potential to create an amazing future for yourself. People are watching you—people see you as a role model whether you like it or not. Nothing would give me more joy than if you take a single idea and use it to build that awesome future.

So you see, your teenage years may feel like the worst time in your life, but you can choose to make them the best. You can shape who you are and what you do. Make some good choices now, and you could set yourself up for some pretty incredible stuff down the road.

If you haven't met me in person, you should know that I love to share and communicate. Find me on Facebook (Yo Yahya) or Twitter (@YahyaBakkar). By reading this book, you're already becoming a part of my family. Read closely. Think. Be honest with yourself. Stay motivated.

Much love and peace,

—Yahya

Chapter 1

Fun

Variety is the Spice of Life!

"*People rarely succeed unless they have fun in what they are doing.*"

–*Dale Carnegie*

Wait, what?

Fun? That's where we're starting? Really?

"But Yahya," you ask, "Shouldn't you start with something serious? Tell me how to make a lot of friends, be successful or get accepted into a prestigious college. Where is the chapter on how to have more money than Jay-Z, more brains than Bill Gates and better abs than Mario Lopez? Isn't fun something—well—for <u>little</u> *kids?*"

Sure is.

But it *should* be for everyone. Having fun is one of the great things about being alive and in this chapter, we'll take a look at why having fun is so important. We'll also analyze why people stop having fun and ways you can gain that fun back.

What is "Fun?"

To me, fun is expressing yourself or doing something that comes from what's inside you. Of course not everyone is the same inside, so not everyone will find the same things fun. Maybe you love an adrenaline rush—so you have fun on roller coasters. If you love to be caught up in a parallel universe, maybe you have fun reading stories or playing video games. If you love competition and pushing your physical and mental limits, you probably like sports. There are hundreds of ways to have fun, but all of them come down to something that speaks to you inside. So find something that you can connect with on a deep, physical or emotional level!

Fun: Express Yourself!

Like I mentioned before, people have different concepts of fun. You might spend a whole day playing World of Warcraft, but your friend thinks it's lame and geeky. Maybe that friend will go hustle down to the court and play some basketball until it's too dark outside to see, but you may think sports are for jocks. You both have fun, but in a different way.

We take our fun personally. The things we enjoy mean a great deal to us because they come from inside. They are things that we connect with. That's why it's super important to be respectful of someone else's idea of fun. Unless it's hurting someone or putting someone down, attempt to understand and embrace that person's idea!

An important thing to remember about the concept of fun; it cannot be forced (although it can be planned). Think about a time you had fun. Did fun happen because you gritted your teeth, flexed your muscles and said "I'm gonna have fun here or else!" Of course not. Fun happens in moments. We're loose, relaxed and "on." Sometimes we plan those moments and sometimes those moments surprise us. Whether fun is planned or a pleasant surprise, you're involved in something that I personally believe is essential to a healthy life. (Along with the other topics in this book, or else this would be a newsletter!)

Now, I have to admit—I'm a little biased. Having fun is one of my goals in life. Sounds weird, right? Well, I don't think it is. I couldn't disagree more with the statement "Fun is a waste of time." Fun is NOT just a little something extra you can include in your life, if you have the time. I believe that having fun is KEY to living a long, healthy and successful life. Let's look at why.

Fun: What's the Big Deal?

When you think about learning, what comes to mind? Textbooks, taking notes, waiting for the bell, long tests and pop quizzes, blah blah blah. But have you ever had a teacher who taught a lesson that was just hands-down, slam-dunk awesome? Where on every level, everyone was engaged? You had fun, the teachers had fun, the class had fun and when the bell rang, you left class understanding something in a new way that notes and review questions could never teach you. Fun and learning are best buddies. (Biffles!)

You see, when we're bored or doing something that eventually gets repetitive, our mind is running on a treadmill, just going forward until the job is done. The mind just wants to get to the end as quickly as possible. But when we are having fun, our mind isn't on a treadmill anymore. It's on a playground. Suddenly, the brain is on the monkey bars, the slide, or jumping off the swings! Your brain still gets the exercise, but it doesn't seem like such a drag. (By the way, I really like playgrounds!)

Fun and learning should be together. All by itself, fun doesn't necessarily *make* you learn, but it can aid in opening up your mind to learning, and make the process of learning much more enjoyable.

Now, you usually can't pick your teachers, and some of them will be booooooooooring. What can you do about it? Well, you can't change the teacher, but you can change your response. Don't let "downer" teachers bring you down too. Don't blame them; just make the best of it and move on.

Remember that not every aspect of someone's life can be fun 24/7. If your teacher has an awesome review game that you love to play, you still have to learn the facts first before playing the game. The message here isn't that school should be like an amusement park, where you run from one crazy ride to the next. The message is that when you're having fun, your mind is open to new experiences and new knowledge, so try to bring a little more fun into your everyday life.

Professor Fun Says . . .

Still don't think that fun is important? Well, I'm not the only one who thinks fun is an important part of our lives. Scientists have been studying the effects of laughter on the body, and here's what they've found. Did you know:

- Laughter relaxes our entire body.
- Laughter boosts our immune system, protecting us against disease.
- Laughter releases endorphins. Endorphins are natural chemicals that our body creates to make us feel happy. So when you laugh, it's actually your hormones that make you feel so good!
- Laughter makes our blood vessels expand and contract, which makes them healthier.
- Laughter is linked to prevention of heart disease. I know heart disease seems like a problem you won't have to worry about for years, but if you make laughter a part of your life now, it can have benefits a long way down the road. Cool!

So Where Does Fun Go?

Think about a timeline of someone's life. When you're a baby, everything is fun and amazing. Just watch a baby look at a funny face, the light shining on the wall or some pretty colors. Then you go to school, play with blocks and sing songs, finger-paint, eat some glue and everything is fun there too.

Then you grow up.

In middle school and high school, all of a sudden you become much more aware of yourself and of others. Your body starts acting strange, other people's bodies start looking very interesting and you are hit with sensory overload. All of a sudden, everyone starts worrying about what others may think, and on that quest to be accepted, suddenly doing fun things isn't as important as doing cool things.

And sometimes, the "cool" things are also pretty stupid things.

If you were like I was when I was a teenager, you wanted to have fun, party and be popular and accepted by your friends. I don't think there's anything wrong with that, but I hate it when people waste their time and potential by getting distracted from living the best life possible. And you know what I mean by distractions: drugs, booze and sex.

For example, I was 13 the first time I got high. I was sitting around in my buddy's basement. People were watching T.V., just hanging out. When we ran out of fun things to do, we got bored. You already know where this is going. I smelled something strange—like a skunk on fire. My buddy Matt handed me something brown and rolled up and said "Take a hit." It was a blunt. I trusted Matt. He was cool, he was down-to-earth and he understood the problems I was having with my family at the time. I took the hit—why not? It looked like it could be fun and it was practically harmless. I mean, at least it was a natural plant.

Imagine a dragon breathing fire down your throat. That's how smoking felt.

Look. I'm not here to point my finger at you and say, "Don't drink! Don't do drugs! Don't socialize with people who do those things!" I've heard adults say that and it just sounds stupid. My goal isn't to tell you what to do; I just want to share my experiences and show you some ways to be creative with your life. The issue isn't about getting high or wasted; it's about you getting distracted by the things that can drag you down in life. In the end, it doesn't even matter if you listen to me or not. What matters is if you listen to *yourself*. Listen closely to that voice that inspires you. I just hope you learn from other people's mistakes because life's too short to make them all on your own.

You've got to know who you are on the inside, or else people and events on the outside can bring you down. Surround yourself with family and friends who want you to have fun. If people who want to get you in stupid situations surround you, you can get pulled down some dangerous paths. Having fun isn't about being stupid; it's about expressing yourself.

Drama: The Fun-Killer

Drama makes for some great T.V. shows. Think of how boring reality T.V. would be with no yelling, no gossiping or slapping people in the face. But drama can do some serious damage to relationships. It hurts other people, and in the end, it will always come back and hurt you too. Drama is addictive, and once you dip your toes in it, it's hard not to dive right in.

Drama will always be around us, and we can't control it. But we can control what we do about it. See, fun is addictive, too. So, next time you hear a rumor about so-and-so, or reeeeeeally want to make fun of someone's stupid new haircut, replace it with a comment that will make people laugh and feel *good*. Drama may be a monster you can never defeat, but you don't have to feed it, either.

MoMENT oF CHALLENGE

Next time you are tempted to spread a rumor or make a not-so-nice comment, stop yourself and replace it with a positive or supportive comment. The truth is, if you have to stoop down low to make fun of someone or talk behind their back, then you probably are jealous, have low self-esteem, or have personal problems that you need to deal with. In other words, you're being a coward and I know you're better than that. Ouch! In your face, but still on your side :)

By the time most people leave high school, fun has taken a back seat to drama. Then you go to college, get a career and family and fun is taken out of the back seat and shoved in the trunk. Achievement—what you accomplish—becomes more important than self-expression. As a result, fun keeps getting pushed back and held off. Suddenly, you look around and you're surrounded by a bunch of miserable adults just like yourself, doing a job because you have to and thinking fun is for little kids.

Sounds terrible!

But for many adults, this is just "normal." It's what "responsible adults do." But you are at a very fortunate time in your life, when you can choose to keep fun as an important part of your daily habits.

Anyone can choose—even the grumpiest, most stuck-in-the-mud adult can choose to change—but when you're young, changing is much easier. So this is my heads-up to you right here, right now—*keep fun in your life.* You'll thank me later.

Today's Homework: Have Fun

Keep it simple. Fun should be, well, fun! You don't need to turn your life upside down to have more of it, either. Here are some quick tips to add more fun into your daily life:

- Go on Youtube and search for your favorite comedian or entertainer. Then watch and laugh! Kevin Hart is my favorite. "Alright, Alright, Alriggghhht!!!" Jeff Dunham is pretty funny too. "I Keeeeeeelllll You!"
- Wear a favorite funny t-shirt. Have a school uniform? Wear the t-shirt underneath. (Pretty cheesy, I know, but it works for some people. Don't hate; appreciate).
- Next time you have a test, don't just sit and stare at your notes. Make flashcards with your friends, and then play a review game.
- Make someone else laugh. The fun will bounce right back to you.
- Invite friends over for a movie party next weekend. It doesn't need to be complicated or expensive—a DVD, popcorn and friends can make for a great night.
- Similarly, throw a game night for friends. It's one thing to play games online, but it's another to have your pals sitting around the kitchen table with you, laughing and playing. And if you think all board games are cheesy, boring and made for old

people, times have changed. For less than $20, you can find some great ones to fit any interest.

- Find 10 songs that make you feel good and make a playlist.
- Exercise. Remember those little chemicals called endorphins that your body releases when you laugh? Well, when you exercise, your body makes *lots* of endorphins, and you feel great after! And who says you need the gym? Not all of us want to be body builders and swim suit models, you can stay active by joining a sports team, or simply playing any game on Wii.
- Smile. Right now, stop reading and smile. It doesn't matter if anyone's looking. Do it. Do it. Seriously, do it. There, feel better?

For whatever reason, "fun" has become something that only little kids can have, that looks irresponsible and is only acceptable if you've gotten all your work done already. I'm not saying you should have fun *instead* of being responsible; I'm saying that having fun is part of being responsible. Having fun helps you take better care of yourself, helps you lift up the people around you, and helps make the world better. Can you think of anything more responsible than that?

Life Lesson #1:

Fun comes from growing, expressing yourself and sharing joyful moments with family and friends. It doesn't come from doing stupid, unhealthy or dangerous things. It also doesn't come from creating drama or feeding into it.

Discussion Questions

1) What is fun?

   _____

   _____

2) Why is it important to respect other people's types of fun?

   _____

   _____

3) What are some of the benefits of having fun?

   _____

   _____

4) What can you do if you have a boring teacher or class?

   _____

   _____

5) How are fun and drama similar? How are they different?

   _____

   _____

6) Agree or Disagree: "It's okay to do something fun even if it puts your health at risk, puts you in danger, or hurts someone else." Discuss.

   _____

   _____

   _____

   _____

CHAPTER 2

Food

You Are What You Eat!

> *"If I put inferior foods in my body today, I'll be inferior tomorrow.*
> *It's that simple."*
>
> *—Jack LaLanne*

Think of a car. Not just any car, like some beat-up old Sedan that you'll replace in a couple years. I'm talking a unique, once-in-a-lifetime ride, a work of art, maybe a brand-new, souped-up Ferrari. Your body is like that car. Food is like gasoline. When you go to the pump to fill up, there are three types of gas you can buy—regular, plus and premium. The premium is the best quality, and will make your engine last a lot longer. It makes sense to put that in the tank of your precious car, right? You wouldn't put the cheapest gas in, and make your car suffer for it. You certainly wouldn't put anything else in the tank, like soda, or toilet water, right? Unfortunately, that's what many of us do to our bodies when we eat junk food.

In this chapter, I won't tell you what to eat. I also won't tell you what not to eat. Those are your choices, but we will talk about why food is important to us and why it's so hard to make good food choices these days. I'm going to expose some of the ugly lies about food, and give you some suggestions for making good food choices. Remember—in this life, you only get one body. Treat it well. So let's get the key in the ignition, hit the gas and go!

Food=Fuel

Food is fuel for our bodies. That is food's main purpose. When it comes down to the science, we eat because food gives us energy. Even the most complex foods break down into some pretty basic building blocks, and each type of block serves a purpose.

**Carbohydrates** _(carbs)_: provide energy

**Proteins**: build muscle tissue

Fats: control body functions

Vitamins and minerals: keep
body tissues healthy

Water: removes waste and keeps
cells working

And that's about it. Obviously, there is a lot more to know about
nutrition, and these categories can be broken down more, but this isn't

health class. For our purposes, you don't need anything more than what's listed here.

Ever hear the old saying, "You are what you eat." It sounds weird, like if I eat tuna, then I turn into a fish, or if I eat banana, I'll become tall, skinny and yellow.

The thing is—that old saying is true.

Pretend you eat a turkey sandwich. You bite into it, chew it and swallow. All those mashed-up foods go into your stomach where they are broken down into nutrients. Then the food passes into your intestines, and the nutrients get absorbed for your body to use. All the nutrients that were once in the turkey sandwich enter our bodies, go into our cells and do jobs. That turkey sandwich literally *becomes* part of your body. Weird!

All That, and a Bag of Potato Chips

Right now, people are becoming overweight and obese at frightening rates. By 2008, about 34% of American adults were considered obese, and 17% of children were obese. Those rates are even higher now, and are much, much higher than they were 40, 30 or even 20 years ago.

So what's so tough about food?

First of all, most of the food we eat has too much sugar, too much fat or loads of nasty chemicals and preservatives that slow us down and make us feel gross.

The obvious solution is to just not eat that disgusting stuff, but it's more complicated than that. That gross stuff is, in most cases, really delicious. In many cases, food that is terrible for our bodies is a blast in our mouths, and we don't want to give those foods up.

But wait. There's more.

Not only are there a lot of unhealthy options out there; we can't even agree on what's healthy versus what's unhealthy. Maybe you've heard of some of these diets: low-fat, low-calorie, low-carb, high-carb, high-protein, organic, vegetarian, vegan, liquid-only, Atkins, South Beach. None of those diets agree on the healthiest ways to eat.

One will say pasta is very healthy, but another says to never touch it. Some say that beef is a terrific source of protein (which it is), but others say it is high in fat and can harm your large intestine (this is also true). There are even ice cream diets, chocolate diets and French fry diets (just look them up!). After a while, it seems *impossible* to make healthy food choices. So why not just tear open the bag of Oreos and go at them with two fists?

Let's start there.

You might think people eat badly because they don't have enough information about nutrition, but actually, the first problem is that we have INFORMATION OVERLOAD. Many well-meaning people will simply give up trying to eat healthy because there is just too much conflicting information about food.

The second difficulty we have with food is that while its main purpose is to fuel our bodies, it serves many other purposes, too. As a result, we end up in some situations that cause us to make poor choices. If all your friends are going out to eat fast food and invite you to join them, it's hard to say no. If your Aunt Grace made an entire apple pie just for you, it'd be rude to turn it down. Occasional treats are fine, but when these treats happen several times a week (or several times a day), they do damage to our bodies.

But the biggest problem we have isn't in our food; it's in our heads. Everyone develops habits; it's human and totally normal. We fall into habits with our daily routine, with studying, with sleep, with the way we act with friends and we have habits for how we eat. After a while, the habit becomes more important than the food itself.

Here's an example. Say your after-school snack is three chocolate chip cookies. On its own, that doesn't sound too bad, until you consider that in an average school year there are 180 school days. This means over that year, you eat 540 cookies, and that doesn't even count treats or special occasions! Those cookies will be a big factor in obesity and if you eat them every day, it just becomes part of the routine, something you don't even think about. You may even *defend* the choice to eat cookies—it was a hard day, the cookies are a reward, you just want to unwind. The thing is, those cookies may taste good in your mouth for a few moments, but they'll clog your body with fat, sugar and preservatives that will make you feel worse in the end.

Lies, Lies, Lies!

Wow. It looks like we have a big task in front of us. Let's start by sorting through this information overload. I'm going to take five common statements—you may have heard them yourself—and blast them apart for the sneaky lies that they are.

Lie #1: There is One BEST Eating Plan Out There.

Face it, if there was a "perfect" plan, then it would've been discovered already. When you're battling that information overload, remember that a lot of people have a lot of different ideas about nutrition, as well as a lot of different goals. You may read about the diet that a movie star used to get huge and bulk up for an action movie, or that a bikini model uses to get super skinny. Elite athletes have their own eating plans. These people, however, are eating for very specific goals—not your goals. Besides, just because you eat like Christian Bale or Megan Fox does not mean you'll *look* like them.

In the end, you have to find your *own* best plan for eating. This is tough. It means trying new foods and new schedules. It means learning a little about nutrition. It means paying attention to how your body responds to what (and when) you eat. For instance, are you feeling more sluggish or more energy? Listen to your body and make your eating choices based on what's best for you, not based on what someone said in a magazine article or blog. It's YOUR body, and the food that goes into it is always YOUR choice.

Lie #2: Food Companies Want You to be Healthy.

Food companies have one goal in mind—to make money. Some of them will make money selling you healthy food, some will make it selling you junk and some will make it selling you junk but making it LOOK healthy. It's not their fault. Companies are just run by people trying to make a living, but it is your responsibility to know what you're putting into your body.

Since healthy eating is a money making machine, companies can use the magic of marketing to make almost anything look healthy. The key word here is LOOK healthy.

For example, soft drinks are some of the worst things to put in your body. They are loaded with extra sugar that just turns into fat. When people started becoming weight-conscious and stopped buying soda, the companies developed "diet" soda, made with fake sweeteners. All of a sudden, it became popular to drink diet sodas because they had no calories, and were supposed to be healthier than regular soda. Well, after a few years, people became worried that the fake sweeteners in diet soda were actually really bad for you, because they're chemicals cooked up in a factory somewhere, and not natural. So companies have started marketing regular old soda as "natural" because it uses "pure sugar," which is just the same old notorious villain, high fructose corn syrup! STAY AWAY!

The same thing has happened with just about every other food product. Some words, like "organic" and "fat-free," have specific nutritional value, but others like "natural" or "diet" or "wholesome" don't necessarily mean a *thing*. Just because a healthy-sounding word is on the box, that does NOT make the food healthy—you have to read the nutrition label and know what you're eating.

MoMENT oF CHALLENGE

Next time you're in the store, find one product that is obviously unhealthy but has packaging to make it LOOK healthy. Good places to start—breakfast cereals, snacks and frozen foods.

Lie #3: If You Look Good on the Outside, You're Healthy Inside.

Obesity gets so much attention these days that it seems like people will do anything to be skinny, but not everyone's body works the same. There are some people who can eat pizza and fries every day and remain thin, while others just walk by a McDonald's and put on five pounds. So if you're naturally skinny, you can eat anything, right?

Here are the basics. If you put junk into your body, it doesn't matter how thin you are, you're still filling your stomach—and every cell of your body—with junk. Thin people can still have heart attacks; get cancer, diabetes, high blood pressure and any number of illnesses caused by food choices. What you put inside you is much more important than how you look outside. Still don't believe me? Ask Dr. Oz. Better yet, Google it.

Lie #4: You Can Eat Whatever You Want When You're Young.

Some adults, based on some very outdated ideas about nutrition, believe that since teens' bodies need lots of food, they can and should eat everything they want to, with no consequences. While there's a kernel of truth in there, most of it is dangerous, misguided wisdom.

It's true—during your teenage years, you grow at a rapid rate. Since your body needs to create energy in order to develop, it needs more calories. It's because of this that teenagers are so famous for eating everything in sight — their bodies *demand* the extra nutrition.

That being said, it's especially important during your teen years to make sure that your body is getting the *right kind* of nutrients. You need important vitamins and minerals that are found only in fruits and vegetables. Filling your cells with toxic chemicals and preservatives can create problems for you down the road. They can even make your life NOW pretty miserable, by making you feel like garbage, physically and mentally.

Also, if you develop a habit of eating badly, those bad eating habits won't just go away when you turn 20 or 30. Adopt good eating habits *now* and live a long and healthy life in the future.

Lie #5: Eating Healthy is Too Hard and Too Expensive.

This is more of a half-truth, half-lie. It's true that nutritious foods are generally more expensive than junk foods. However, the difference is not as bad as you'd expect. Make replacements. Next time "ice cream" is on the grocery list, replace it with "apples" or "grapes." You'll see that you still have something sweet to eat, and you'll hardly notice the difference in your wallet. Think of it this way, too—would you rather pay a little extra now for healthy food, or a LOT more down the road in the doctor's office when you're suffering from heart disease and high blood pressure?

As for being too difficult, it really isn't, once you learn the basics. In the next section, I'll help you with those basics. Again, I'm NOT going to tell you what to eat and not eat, but I'll point out some strategies. Sound good?

Making the Fridge Your Friend: Tips for Healthier Eating

First of all, I want to repeat two important points about eating:

1) Your eating plan should be YOUR eating plan. Find what's best for you and your body.
2) Do research and be knowledgeable. Understand what foods are good sources of carbs, of proteins and of fats. Learn to read nutrition labels. Learn what a "serving size" means. Knowing the basics will help you wade through the information overload.

Yes, there is a lot of confusing, mixed-up information out there. However, there are a few principles that most nutritionists agree on. So without further ado, here are four tips for making good food choices:

Tip #1: Focus on Produce

"Produce" refers to fruits and vegetables. Generally, if it grew in the ground or on a tree, it's good for you. Just don't do drugs or I'll come over there and karate kick you.

How can you eat more fruits and veggies? Make replacements. Rather than eating those three cookies when you get home from school, have an apple with peanut butter. Have a salad at dinner. Sneak vegetables into your food anywhere you can—lettuce and tomato on sandwiches, strawberries in yogurt, bananas in cereal. It's easier than you think. You will feel better, think clearly and have WAY more energy.

Tip #2: Go Organic When Possible

You'd be amazed at the poison that is in some of your food. We're talking toxic chemicals that you'd never dream of eating if you knew they were on your plate. One of the best ways to protect yourself from these poisons is to eat organic food whenever possible.

Organic plants have to be grown without any pesticides or chemical fertilizers. Animals are organic only if they were raised on an organic diet themselves, were not genetically engineered, and were not pumped full of steroids, growth hormones or antibiotics.

Why would farmers use these chemicals in their business? Same reason food companies use sneaky marketing tactics—money. Consumers want to eat big, meaty chicken breasts and bananas as long as baseball bats. Fertilizers, pesticides, antibiotics and steroids make foods bigger and more attractive. Unfortunately, all those toxic chemicals stay inside the food, and when you eat the food, you eat the chemicals, too. Gross.

Tip #3: Shop the Perimeter

Picture a typical grocery store. Most of them have the same layout. What's on the outside aisles? Usually produce, meats and dairy. What will you find in the inner aisles? Boxed cereals, pre-packaged meals, cookies, chips, candy and more. In general, the stuff lining the outer walls of the grocery store is better for you than the other stuff. This is a good general principle.

Tip #4: Foods to Limit

Just as there are some foods that most people agree are good for you, there are some that don't really belong in any healthy diet:

- **Too much fat.** Fats are critical to our health, but only in small amounts. High-fat foods not only make us fat; they also clog our arteries which puts a strain on our hearts.
- **Too much sugar.** Sugars are a form of carbohydrates—which we need—but a lot of products have *added* sugar that our bodies don't need. If your body doesn't need it, it stores the sugar as fat. It can also cause a ton of cavities, energy problems and make you more susceptible to diabetes. Oh and watch out for corn syrup, high-fructose corn syrup and any word on a nutrition label that ends in "-ose." They're all different words for sugar, my friend.
- **Too much salt**. This is a sneaky one, because salt is eeeeverywhere. Now, salt is a mineral our body needs, but again, too much is a bad thing. Too much salt is linked with many health problems, and also causes us to gain weight due to water retention. A healthier alternative is sea salt or Celtic

salt. The difference between real salt and iodized salt is that real salt isn't processed. That means all the minerals are in there for you to absorb. If it came in a box or a bag, can be cooked in the microwave or is a frozen dinner or snack, look at "sodium" on the nutrition label. I'll bet there's a big scary number next to it.

- **Preservatives**. Preservatives are chemicals that are used to keep food from going bad. For example, real cheese has to be refrigerated to keep from spoiling, but if you buy a box of macaroni and cheese, that cheese can sit on the shelf for weeks (or months, or years)! Why? Preservatives!

- **In general**, the shorter the list of ingredients, the better the food is for you.

- **Think about this**, if you can't pronounce it, don't eat it. Chips may have "whole corn" and "skim milk" in them, but they also have "sodium acetate," "disodium inosinate" and "disodium guanylate." Do you know what those are? Me neither. Steer clear.

This chapter is not supposed to make you feel down, guilty or scared, but it should make you more aware. Healthy eating isn't a drag. It isn't a chore. It's a key to living a long and happy life. Without your health, you have *nothing*. You can't have fun with your family, you can't make money and you can't spend time doing the things you want to do.

The idea to take away from this chapter is this: *be aware of what you put in your body*. I'm not saying to never eat anything unhealthy ever again. Even super-fit athletes will eat a slice of cake at a birthday party, or have some pizza with their friends. It's not what you eat once in a while, it's your *habits* that will make or break your health. So, start today by changing just one habit. Put down the potato chips, grab a handful of baby carrots and rev up your engines as you head down the highway to a healthier you.

Life Lesson #2:

The things you eat affect the way you feel and grow. Choosing a particular eating plan isn't as important as choosing foods that make you feel better and healthier in the long run.

Discussion Questions

1) **What is the main purpose of food?**

   _____

   _____

2) **Explain why it's important to care about what you eat and drink.**

3) **The problem isn't that we don't have enough information about nutrition; the problem is that we have_____**

   _____.

4) **Explain why foods that appear to be good for you may not actually be healthy.**

5) **What are a few things you can do to improve your eating habits?**

   _____

   _____

6) Agree or disagree: "Food companies should be punished for tricking customers into thinking their food is healthy." Discuss.

_____

_____

_____

_____

CHAPTER 3

Fitness

Be Fit or Die!

"Those who think they have no time for bodily exercise will sooner or later have to find time for illness."

—*Edward Stanley*

I magine you have to go out to the store (to buy some healthy snacks like we talked about in Chapter 2). It's not far, but it's a little too far to walk, so you decide to bike there. Tires are full and the brakes seem good. You climb on, and the first couple of pedals take some extra effort.

Would you stop then?

Say you don't stop. You overcome that initial push and get into a nice rhythm. You ride to the end of the street, but you're still not at the store yet.

Would you stop then?

After a couple blocks, you feel a tingle in your legs. Your muscles, which had been sitting on the couch for the past two hours (maybe most of your life), are waking up. You're "feeling the burn."

Would you stop, get off the bike, leave it in the road and quit then?

It sounds ridiculous, but this is a pretty accurate description of our relationship with exercise. There are a thousand excuses to not do it, and most people are pretty good at making all of them—including myself at times. Well, throw out your excuses and get ready because I'm going to unleash the nerd in me. Check this out, the Center for Disease Control recommends that all adults get at least 30 minutes of exercise each day. Do you know how many do that? Only 35% of them, and 33% say they NEVER exercise. That's pretty scary. You know what's scarier? Most people won't even "get on the bike" in the first place. What are their excuses?

- The store is too far away. I'll never get there.
- I just don't have the body type that can ride bikes.
- What if I get hurt going to the store?
- I could go to the store, but there's something really good on T.V. Maybe I'll go later, or tomorrow or next week.

- I'm big-boned. If I get on that bike, the tires will go flat. No way!

Teenagers live lots of different lifestyles with lots of different fitness levels. Maybe you are already an athlete and love that feeling of sweating, pushing yourself and achieving. This chapter still will have some new ideas for you. Maybe you exercise occasionally—a game of basketball, swimming in the pool in the summer, but nothing regular. This chapter will show you how to make exercise a regular part of life. And for those of you who are really frustrated with exercise, with your body image and with your self-esteem—and you are NOT alone—this chapter will help you see why exercise is great, what stops people from doing it and how you can get on the bike, even if you THINK you'll hate it. In the end, you'll learn to love it.

Why is Fitness Great?

Ask 50 people what they think about fitness and exercise, and you'll get 50 different answers. Some people love it. Others exercise once in a while but wish they could do more. And there are plenty of people who have had bad experiences with exercise, and don't want to try it ever again. They just don't see the *point*. Well, let's talk about it. Why would anyone want to get off their comfy couch, put on sneakers and go run around or lift a bunch of heavy weights? Here are four great reasons:

1) Your Health

Remember last chapter, when we talked about how you get just one life and one body, so take care of it? Same thing applies here. Some people worry about damaging their bodies with exercise, but I'll tell you what—*the most damaging thing you can do to your body is to NOT use it.* Physical activity protects your body from many of the problems that affect millions of people—obesity, heart disease and high blood pressure, just to name a few. Think of it this way: humans are animals, and animals' bodies are made to do some pretty tough stuff. It might feel weird to start exercising after sitting around for a long time, but you're actually doing things the human body was designed to do.

2) Stress Relief

Does school get you frustrated and mad? How about your friends and their drama? How about your parents? Your siblings? A boyfriend or girlfriend? Someone picking on you? *Everyone* feels stress. How we deal with that stress will determine a lot about us. How do you relieve stress? Do you zone out and watch T.V.? Do you dominate in Call of Duty? Do you text your friends? Do you have a drink or smoke a cigarette? Do you blast loud music? Reading also works, but you're already doing that. Kudos! There are many ways to relieve stress, but working out is one of the healthiest and most effective.

Everyone knows that stress is mentally tiring—you feel worn out, your brain locks onto the problem and all your thoughts turn negative. But there are also physical effects of stress. When your body feels threatened (stressed out), it releases a chemical called cortisol. If you don't flush the cortisol from your body, it accumulates, leads to weight gain, weakens your immune system and makes you feel run down. Sitting around, playing video games and smoking or drinking may ease your mind for a bit, but it doesn't do anything to help your body—in fact, it will make your body sicker. Exercise is one of only a few stress relievers that clears your mind AND your body.

3) Self-discovery

Whoa, Yahya. Self-discovery? We're getting kind of heavy here.

It isn't heavy. It's serious, but nothing to be afraid of. Let me explain. Okay, maybe I can't. It's not something that can be explained. It has to be experienced.

Read the testimony of an athlete who puts him or herself through extreme physical trials. Marathon runners, power lifters, mountain climbers, they all say something in common—that when you push yourself to the very limits of your capabilities, you discover who you really are.

Figuring out your identity is a key part of your teenage years. Friends and family will tell you who you are, society will tell you and you will tell yourself. If you want to find out what you're truly made of, exercise is one path to that discovery.

Now before you freak out, you don't have to be an elite athlete to find yourself. In fact, every time you work out, from the very FIRST workout, you can find out what you're made of. For example, if you think you can't run, go out and try, and make it all the way to the end of the block. You've just discovered something about yourself that you never knew! Next time, you'll push yourself further. In a year, you'll be running 10 miles, and when you don't think you can go to 11, you do. It's a constant journey. Finding and breaking your boundaries is necessary to grow as a person.

4) Gain Respect

Just from exercise?

Sure!

But why?

Maybe our society is all about image, and we judge people on how they look. Maybe it goes back to that "humans are animals" thing. In the wild, animals respect the strongest and fittest of their kind, and maybe humans are the same way.

But I think it's something more. When you discover yourself, you gain a new, inner confidence. Your insecurities and fears dissolve away when you have a clearer sense of who you really are. This inner confidence will show to the outside world. So by including fitness in your lifestyle, you won't just look and feel better, you'll be stronger on the inside, and people will notice. You'll see value in yourself, and then people will see value in you as well. Remember—if you don't see value in yourself, why should anyone else? It's as simple as that. You'll become an example of strength, commitment and inspiration to those around you, and that is a seriously awesome way to live.

Yeah, but—

So exercise is great. Then why are so many people *avoiding* it?

Good question. Remember the biggest roadblock people have when it comes to eating right?

INFORMATION OVERLOAD

We have the same problem with exercise.

Go to Google. Put in "weightlifting" or "aerobic" or "gaining muscle" or "burn fat." You will get so many hits that you could never read every article, even if you read for the rest of your life. On top of that, those articles will contain a lot of conflicting information. How much should I run? How far? How fast? Can I get injured? How can I build lots of muscle fast? I want to look like Arnold Schwarzenegger in 1982— how do I do it? Some of it will be from "experts," and some of it will be from every-day people. Some people know what they're talking about, and many don't. Sorting out the experts from all the rubbish can get to be overwhelming.

But fear not my fellow grasshopper, there's a better way. Notice the **patterns.** People start exercising all the time, but they give up all the time, too. It usually follows the same pattern:

Step 1) **Frustration**: "I hate looking like this! I want to be huge/ripped/skinny/smoking hot."

Step 2) **Enthusiasm**: "That's it! I'm going to start weightlifting/running/swimming/playing basketball TODAY."

Step 3) **Initial High**: "That first workout felt awesome! I'm on my way!"

One week later

Step 4) **Frustration Part II:** "I've only lost one pound! How long is this going to take?"

Two weeks later

Step 5)   **Surrender:** "Forget this! I hardly see a change. I guess I'll always be too skinny/too weak/too fat/too ugly."

Sound familiar?

In our culture, we want results, and we want them now. Someone inspires us who is really fit and we want to look like him or her right away. Unfortunately, that's just not realistic. You see if you've gotten stuck in a rut and exercise hasn't been part of your life in a while (or ever), you can't just reverse years of inactivity like that. If it took you 15 years to become overweight, is it fair to think you'll get in shape in 15 days?

We all know that motivation is important. For exercise, what's your motivation? For many people, it doesn't go any further than body image.

Unfortunately, if your goal is only skin deep, you may be setting yourself up for failure. Don't get me wrong—wanting to look good is a great goal. If we feel better about our looks, we tend to be more confident and happier. However, if your ONLY goal is the way you look, then your motivation will fizzle away in a few weeks. Don't exercise for other people, or to get noticed. Do it for you. Remember—the results won't come quickly. Results = Consistency + Commitment. Bodybuilders, models, athletes and movie stars work for years to achieve their results. Few people can stay motivated over that much time with no other goal than physical appearance. Their goals have to be deeper.

Think of it this way. Motivation comes from INSIDE, so to stay motivated, the results can't be only on the OUTSIDE. To go back to the bike metaphor (yeah, metaphors, just like in English class), motivation is what keeps you pedaling.

Another problem that hurts people's motivation is called the *plateau*. A plateau is a feature in geography; it's a hill with sloping sides but a flat top. The term is used as a metaphor (that word again!) for fitness goals. Our fitness goals ALWAYS hit plateaus. We start out strong and see results. Then, over time, we stop seeing changes, even if we're doing the same workout. This lack of progress makes people feel frustrated, and they give up.

For example, let's say you exercise by running. At first, you couldn't run at all, but after some hard work you were able to complete a full mile. It took 15 minutes, but you did it. Your long-term goal is to run a mile in six minutes. You kept running and improving your time, down to 12 minutes, then 10, then nine. And then suddenly, you couldn't run faster than a nine-minute mile. You push and push but never go any faster. That's a plateau. Does it make sense to just stop trying?

Of course not, but that's what many people do. When the results don't match the effort, it's tempting to give up. ***Don't give up!*** If you keep pushing your maximum effort, as well as mix in new forms of exercise, eventually you'll break through that plateau and set new records for yourself.

Do you remember what I said earlier about excuses? *Life will give you as many excuses as you need to keep you from getting in shape.* Don't let it. Short of having a medical condition that prevents you from exercising, any "reason" to not get exercise is only an excuse. Exercise can be as extreme or as gentle as you need for your lifestyle. For most people, the hardest step in a fitness plan is the first step. Using the bike metaphor, we're talking about the people who won't even get on the bike. They give excuses why they can't/won't/shouldn't/don't want to go to the store, but in the end, they're still out of milk.

MoMENT oF CHALLENGE

Give Yourself a Basic Physical Fitness Test

- How far can you run without stopping? _____
- How many pushups can you do in a row? _____
- How many pull-ups can you do in a row? _____
- Can you touch your toes without bending your knees? _____
- How many days each week do you exercise? _____

My Fitness Story

In my own life, I've stayed fit in a lot of different ways, based on what I needed at the time and on what felt right for me. I practiced martial arts—Taekwondo, specifically—starting around age 11. I did that for many years, and then when I left, I kept strong by doing pushups and using a pair of dumbbells. It's amazing how much you can do with just a few basic exercises!

Then when I met a trainer who showed me some basic weightlifting exercises, I learned about the importance of form. While keeping good form is a constant process—no one gets it exactly right the first time—it is critical to use good form to minimize your chance of injury and maximize your results. If you're interested to learn more about proper form, go to Youtube.com and search "proper form for (INSERT EXERCISE)." That should help you.

After that, I really got into weightlifting. I actually got really big—I weighed about 195 pounds at 5'7 with 14% body fat! But I wasn't eating right, and while I was strong, I didn't feel healthy. After cleaning up my diet, I slimmed down, and incorporated body weight exercises like Pilates and yoga. Now, all those different forms of exercise are part of my life and me. I feel strong AND healthy, and that's huge.

In reality, this entire book is about fitness. Not just physical fitness, but mental and emotional fitness, as well. Having a strong, sharp mind and having a healthy, balanced emotional life are as important as being in good shape. Mental health and emotional health are each also closely connected to your physical health. If you're stressed emotionally, your physical health suffers. If your body isn't healthy, your mind isn't clear. All the different aspects of your life are connected to one another so take care of yourself in all the different ways you can.

In the next section, I'm going to talk about some of the flat-out lies about fitness that keep getting in the way of achieving health. Many of these lies are the very excuses people use to avoid exercise.

MORE Lies, Lies, Lies!

Lie #1: There is one "Best" Fitness Plan Out There.

Sound familiar? It's the same lie that exists in the food world. Every workout will claim to be the "best" or the "ultimate" or the "only workout you'll ever need." The companies that design these workouts are trying to win your business, not give you the straight and honest truth. The straight and honest truth is that there are hundreds of ways to exercise, and there is no one, best way. For best results, try lots of different forms of exercise. Mix it up!

Lie #2: I Can't Afford to Exercise.

The fitness industry makes billions of dollars each year, selling gym memberships, fancy home gyms, cutting-edge workout DVDs and pieces of equipment that look like medieval torture devices. Do you need all these to start?

Not at all. There are so many ways to exercise that require no equipment at all! If you have a pair of sneakers, a ball or a jump rope, you can burn fat and lose weight. Want to build strength? Pushups, pull-ups, dips and crunches are all powerful bodyweight exercises that require little or no equipment. Get creative. Go to the playground, go to the monkey bars and do a couple of chin-ups (don't kick little kids off if they were there first, though. Be nice!). Lack of money is not a reason to avoid exercise; it's only an excuse.

Lie #3: I'll Never Have the Time to Work Out!

This is a lie that both teens and adults buy into. In today's very busy world, carving out hours of time just for sweating doesn't just seem pointless; it seems flat-out impossible.

But when you're starting a fitness routine, you don't need hours a day, 15 or 20 minutes will be challenging enough. Sneak in your workouts by getting up a few minutes earlier in the morning or doing them right after school. Do pushups and crunches right before bed. If you want more advanced results, you might need up to an hour a day, but no one *needs* more than that.

Lie #4: But I Saw This Infomercial for an Easy Workout to get Killer Abs!

I'm sure you've seen these infomercials. Usually they feature some super-skinny swimsuit model or He-Man looking dude, using some contraption and smiling (but not sweating). *Perfect abs in just eight minutes a day! Lose 20 pounds this week, just with this one pill! The easiest, most effective workout you'll <u>ever</u> try.*

Ahh, the power of advertising. Those ads are sending some inaccurate ideas to you; don't believe them. First of all, the actors they have in these advertisements look so good because they have worked *very hard* to look like that. One piece of equipment is NOT going to be solely responsible for that rockin' bod.

And look—I just said fitness can be very simple, and doesn't cost much, and doesn't have to take up your life but I *didn't* say it would be easy. If it were so easy, everyone would be doing it already. There will be times when you're sweaty and uncomfortable and doubting you can go on. But that's where you grow, and learn and discover yourself. If a workout is easy, then you're probably not working out hard enough.

Lie #5: I'm a Guy/Girl. I Can't Do THAT!

I'm going to split this one into two discussions: one for the ladies, and one for the gents.

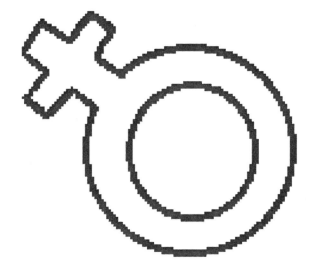

LADIES: In general, women tend to be more interested in burning fat and getting toned. Most are not interested in getting "huge" and "ripped." As a result, they tend to focus on aerobics and fat-burning workouts. However, they also fear looking like a bodybuilder, all bulky with veins popping out, so they *avoid* strength training (free weights, weight machines, pushups and pull-ups).

This is a big mistake. Strength and resistance training is key to your health and physique. Lifting some weights will NOT make you look like a she-man. Those few women who are competitive body builders did not get to look that way by accident. They have highly specialized training, diet and often hormone therapies.

In fact, adding some muscle-building activities into your workout will *improve* your figure. Think of it this way: When men build muscle, it makes them look more masculine. When women build muscle, it makes them look more feminine.

GENTS: Men, on the other hand, tend to try and become more muscular (this is a generalization, of course). "Muscle culture" has become very popular since the 1980s, and countless movies, magazines and websites glamorize huge, ripped dudes.

First of all, many of those images don't give us an accurate idea of what strength is, so take some time and think about what's more important: for you to look like "The Situation" from *The Jersey Shore,* or to be able to lift your own body up from the floor, or to be able move a heavy piece of furniture.

Men also sometimes dismiss "girly" forms of exercise like Yoga. Let me tell you, Yoga is a lot harder than it looks. Yoga is an ancient tradition from India, and has been practiced by millions of men throughout the ages. There is absolutely nothing girly about it, and in fact the first time—or first several times—you try it, you may find yourself drenched in sweat and struggling to keep up. Yoga will increase your flexibility and strength, bring you a sense of stability in life, and physically and mentally challenge you like no other exercise.

Overall, for both men and women, remember this: there is no such thing as exercise for men or for women. The human body is the human body, regardless of sex and what it craves is to be challenged. Go out there and challenge it.

What Can I Do?

In any fitness program, one of the keys is to be informed. Know your stuff. Research can be tricky because of the information overload, but if you find reputable websites or books, they'll be good guides. Just beware of anything that suggests something drastic and radical; it might not be trustworthy.

Another good place to start is to seek the advice of someone who knows more than you do. Not only will they probably be a trustworthy teacher, but you'll also be more comfortable with them. For example, I know a lot about fitness and working out. My 15-year-old little brother is starting to work out, and is curious about how to get bigger. My advice is closer to his heart (and probably less expensive!) than what he'd get from a personal trainer.

Are you not sure where to start? Not sure what "fitness" even means? This will break it down:

#1 Long-term Health

What is it? Lower stress, blood pressure, risk of heart disease and diabetes with a stronger immune system.

Why is it important? You'll live a long time, feel healthy and strong and gain confidence.

How to practice it? Exercise! In any form! (See below). Eat healthy foods, relax, love and have fun.

#2 Flexibility

What is it? The distance your joints can move.

Why is it important? Protects you from injury, slows aging.

How to practice it? Stretching, Yoga and Pilates.

#3 Strength

What is it? The amount of force your muscles can exert.

Why is it important? Bigger muscles and stronger bones.

How to practice it? Weightlifting, bodyweight exercises (pushups, pull-ups, etc.)

#4 Endurance

What is it? Ability your body has to keep going over a long time.

Why is it important? Burn fat, stronger lungs.

How to practice it? Run, swim, martial arts, box, bike and jump rope.

Final Thoughts:

I know this probably feels like a lot of information, suggestions, warnings and confusing ideas. Let me boil this whole chapter down into two words:

DO SOMETHING!

Maybe I've inspired you to become an Olympic power lifter. If so, great. Maybe you want to run a marathon someday. Awesome! Now go out and get some weights, or start running. Don't just think. Do. Maybe my words have convinced you to change your life just a little. Maybe you want to start going for a 20-minute walk when you get home from school. Terrific! Now do it. To me—and more importantly, to your health—*what* you do for exercise isn't as important as *you doing something.* Anything. A little exercise is better than none.

Life Lesson #3:

Stop making excuses for yourself. Do a form of exercise that you love and that doesn't feel like a chore. Dancing is an exercise. Wii Fit is an exercise. So challenge yourself and discover who you really are. And remember, life will give you all the reasons you need to limit your potential. Don't let it.

Discussion Questions

1) **Describe four benefits of physical fitness.**

   _____

   _____

2) What are some of people's fears about exercise, and why are they false fears?

_____

_____

3) Explain the difference between fitness being simple and fitness being easy.

4) What traps do women fall into when it comes to exercise? What about men?

_____

_____

5) Describe your own level of physical fitness: fanatical, casual, occasional or never in a million years.

   a. What form(s) of exercise do you practice?

_____

_____

   b. How could you improve your habits?

_____

_____

6) Why is it important to build flexibility, strength AND endurance?

_____

_____

7) Agree or disagree: "The hardest part of exercising is starting." Discuss.

_____

_____

_____

_____

CHAPTER 4
Fashion
It's About Attitude!

"Be sure of what you want and be sure about yourself. Fashion is not just beauty; it's about good attitude. You have to believe in yourself and be strong."

—Adriana Lima

It. Whatever "it" is, you know you've got to have it. Maybe it's sneakers or a jacket. Maybe it's a cute pair of jeans, a funky hat or a hilarious t-shirt. Maybe you've been thinking about it, eyeing it in magazines, online or in the store window until it takes up all your thoughts. Or maybe you were just out shopping, and there it was on the rack, with a chorus of angels and a beam of sunlight, and you knew right then you couldn't leave the store without it.

Fashion.

Work It, Work It, and Turn!

Now, by the way, for this chapter, "fashion" doesn't mean runways, chiseled models and bizarre dresses that no one would actually wear. When I'm talking about fashion here, I mean using the way you dress to express yourself, and that's something everyone does.

"Wait, hold up! Not me!" you might be saying. "I don't buy popular stuff just to fit in. My style is unique, and I don't care about fashion." Or maybe you're saying, "Fashion is just for shallow people who only care about looking good. I just wear any old shirt and sneakers, but I don't really have a fashion."

Guess what? You do. I like to call it "style."

Some people get a lot of pleasure out of following the trends and dressing in the hottest new styles. They love the creativity of buying and discovering outfits. Some people want to make their own, unique statement with what they wear. And some people just throw on any old thing and aren't that concerned at all about appearance. All of these are different ways of expressing yourself through the way you dress, such as:

- The coolest styles can increase your confidence and make you feel more "put-together."
- Retro, offbeat or quirky clothes can show your individual style and make you stand out.
- Funny t-shirts reveal your sense of humor and will draw eyes— and laughs—to you.
- Sports jerseys advertise your team pride. Same goes for band t-shirts.
- Subtle, understated clothes show that you are confident in who you are, and don't need a unique style of dress to feel good about yourself.

Take me, for example. Some motivational speakers dress in suits and ties, and I thought about doing that, but you know what? That's not me. I wear clothes that make me feel comfortable, and make me feel like me. That's the power of fashion!

But Who Cares?

For every person who's really into clothing and style, there's another who just doesn't care. Maybe this is you. Maybe you feel like fashion is just something that shallow, rich people worry about, getting hung up on appearances. Maybe you think fashion is fake.

Remember our definition at the beginning of the chapter? Fashion is about more than clothes; it's about expressing who you are through the way you dress. Fashion isn't fake at all; at its best, fashion is an outside presentation of our true personalities and interests.

Two people in my life who care a lot—and know a lot—about fashion are my girlfriend, Kate, and my good friend Osama. I asked each of them what's important about fashion, and look at what they both agree on:

Kate: "Sometimes people will judge us based on our outside appearance. It doesn't matter what other people think. The important thing is that we feel good about ourselves."

Osama: "From the first glance, people look at other people. They see what they're wearing, and that's how they define them, so it's important to make that first impression. Fashion does that."

Ever heard of the expression "don't judge a book by its cover?" Guess what? It happens. People judge us—and we judge others—*all the time.* Is it right? No. Does it happen? Yes.

Let's say two people apply for a job at a high-powered financial company. Both of them are equally qualified and have similar experience. One arrives for his interview in a suit and tie, while the other has a lip ring and combat boots. Who will get hired? Nine times out of 10, the guy in the suit. Is that fair? Maybe not, maybe Mr. Lip Ring will be a much better employee, but his fashion expressed a sense of rebelliousness and defiance that just won't fly in the business world. Now if they were applying for a job in a guitar shop, that's a different story!

The point is, while you may not be interested in fashion, and may not see the point in it, people will judge you by the way they see you. If you aren't conscious of what your appearance says about you, people may treat you in ways you don't understand.

MoMENT oF CHALLENGE

Stop reading, go find a mirror and look at yourself. What do you think your clothes say about you? How would you describe your style? Make sure you don't judge yourself. Just observe your style without any emotion or resentment to it.

My Fashion Story

When I was in 5th grade, I was a pretty normal kid with a few friends and I felt pretty good about myself. Cliques don't really exist yet, not like they do when you get older.

Then in 6th grade, I moved to a new school. I didn't fit in or know anyone. On top of that, right before school started, I broke three of my toes on my left foot and had it in a big old cast. So I had that working against me in my new school. Now I don't know if you've ever had to wear a cast on your foot, but it's heavy. And one thing that's really hard to do is shower. I admit—I would sometimes go two or three days without a shower, just because it was so hard with that cast on. So here I am, new kid in school, wearing the same shorts and tee shirts I was wearing to 5th grade, in a clunky foot cast and not showered. The kids teased me, called me "stinky" and generally made fun of me.

Fast forward to 8th grade. I went from awkward (and a little smelly) to being voted *Best Dressed* in my class. Pretty cool, right?

Then I went to high school, and something went wrong. My sense of fashion stopped being about being me. It started being about trends and pop stars. I listened to Lil' Wayne, and I dressed like Lil' Wayne. I listened to techno, and I wore tight jeans and shades. I was losing sense of who I was (you'll be reading more about that in the upcoming chapters) and it showed in the way I dressed.

Now, I have a much better sense of myself, and it shows. I dress pretty simply—jeans and a shirt. I don't feel the need to impersonate other people or follow trends because I know who I am and what I stand for. I don't consider myself a "fashion guy," but the clothes I wear reflect my inner confidence.

Traps!

The world of fashion can lead us down some dangerous paths. What should be healthy, fun and expressive can become shallow, obsessive or misleading if taken the wrong ways. Watch out for:

- Letting your clothes define you

Being concerned with fashion is great, but never forget—you are you, you are not your clothes. When you cross the line from "I love these pants—they are SO me!" to "I have to wear This-or-That Brand Jeans or I'm nothing," you've gone too far.

Remember—you are <u>you</u> underneath your clothes. If you don't have a clear sense of who you are before you get dressed, it's not fair to expect other people to see beyond your appearance. Think of it this way: we all may be of different races and skin colors, but we have individual identities underneath. We also have different styles of dressing, but our inner personalities go beyond the clothes we wear. You wouldn't judge someone based on his or her race, so don't judge someone based on his or her style of dress, either.

- Following the herd

This is especially hard during your teen years, because fitting in is so important. *Here is the thing to remember—"fitting in" should mean finding a group of friends who like you for who you are. If the only thing you have in common with your friends is the brand of sneakers you wear, it might be time to reevaluate your friendships.* Oh and by the way, being different or "weird" is okay! That's what sets you apart from the crowd! It makes you UNIQUE! It's like what Justin Timberlake said on the Ellen DeGeneres show: "The thing that makes you different today, is the thing that will make you sexy later on." He was talking about his nose. Think about it, would you rather look at a thousand black and white cows or one awesome purple cow? Would you rather look at a hundred white eggs or one bright orange egg? Maybe the better question is: why would you want to look at cows and eggs in the first place? Good question. I have no answer.

- Blaming school uniforms

Yeah, uniforms can be a drag. They're usually not very stylish, and many people feel that uniforms prevent students from expressing their individuality.

Well, yeah, that's the point. Schools require uniforms for a lot of reasons—security, preventing discrimination and boosting school spirit.

But don't let it get you down! Remember—you are NOT your clothes. No uniform is going to change who you are. So go ahead, wear your uniform with school pride, and be yourself. Besides, you can wear what you want on weekends!

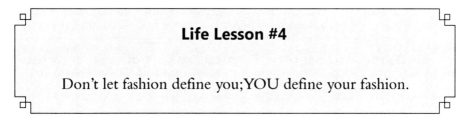

Life Lesson #4

Don't let fashion define you; YOU define your fashion.

Discussion Questions

1) **Explain how people who don't care about fashion are impacted by it.**

2) Think about a time you were judged based on your appearance.

   a. How did it make you feel?

   _____

   _____

   b. Do you think that person's judgment was accurate?

   _____

   _____

3) Think of a time you judged someone on his/her appearance.

   a. Even if you didn't say anything to that person, how did your judgment affect what you thought of him or her?

   _____

   _____

4) Describe a situation when "following the herd" could be pointless or even dangerous.

5) What are some ways you can express yourself, even if you have to wear school uniforms?

   _____

   _____

6) Agree or Disagree: "Fashion is a part of everyone's life." Discuss.

   _____

   _____

   _____

   _____

CHAPTER 5
Fallacies
Buying Into Labels

"*Labels are for filing. Labels are for clothing. Labels are not for people.*"

—*Martina Navratilova*

Sticks and stones may break my bones, but words will never hurt me. You heard that saying before, right? Some people call it a great little tidbit of wisdom for living our lives.

I call it *ignorance*. Sorry grandma.

Let me ask you this: Think of a time when you broke a bone or twisted a joint. It may have hurt at the time, but does it still hurt you now? Probably not.

Now think of something hurtful someone said to you once. Can you still feel the sting of that injury? I bet you can.

The truth is, words are not meaningless or empty. Just because they have no weight doesn't mean they can't crush you, and just because they have no heat doesn't mean they can't fill you with the fire of inspiration. Words matter. Words are powerful. Words can uplift someone's life or derail it. Let's look at how words—specifically the hurtful labels people use—can affect the way you view yourself.

Tell Me, Who are You?

I want you to think about yourself. (It's okay. You're not being conceited; you're reflecting). Think about some of the qualities that describe and define you. Are you smart? Are you popular? Creative? Shy? A poor student? Cool? A troublemaker? Lazy? Athletic? Dumb? These are just some of the ways people describe themselves.

Now that you have two or three words to describe yourself, I want you to think about *why* they describe you. How do you know you're smart? In what way are you lazy? What does being "cool" look like?

Now I want you to think way back. Can you remember when you first identified with those qualities? Who first told you that you were a troublemaker? At what point did you become an athlete? Have you always known you were creative, or did someone tell you that you were?

Now, for the really hard task. Think about each of those qualities that describe you. Do they really describe who you know yourself to be now, or do they describe:

- Who you used to be?
- Who you would like to be?
- Who someone told you that you are?

This chapter is called **Fallacies: Buying Into Labels** because so much of what we believe about ourselves is based on *untrue things that other people tell us*. Sometimes our beliefs aren't based on fact or truth or self-knowledge, they're based on the misperceptions, disappointments, expectations and illusions of the people in our lives. Parents, siblings, teachers, coaches and friends all try to put you into a category. A parent tells his or her child he is smart, so the child believes it. A parent says,

77

"You're too stupid to do well in school," so the child believes it. Little kids are like sponges for words—they soak in eeeeverything.

School cliques form this way too. "Look at the nerds over there, being all nerdy and everything" or, "You only hang out with the other guys from the basketball team, so you're a jock."

Why do these labels exist? Well, for one, labels make things convenient. If your binder is labeled, you find what you need more easily. Can you imagine a store with no labels on the shelves? Labeling people makes it much easier to figure out who that person is and where he or she belongs. However, labels are convenient for the labeler but rarely for the labeled. If you've ever been unfairly tagged as one kind of person, did it make your life better?

Another reason is insecurity. Some people feel more confident in themselves when they identify other people, label them, point out what makes them unique, and not in a nice way. I remember one incident my freshman year of high school when this happened to me.

Story Time!

I was in English class, sitting in the front of the room. A girl named Sam sat a couple rows over. She had a punk rocker style that I thought was really hot. I had a crush on her. How did I show it? The usual way—I joked around, showed off, stared at her without *looking* like I was staring at her. You know what I'm talking about, right? Well, I was laughing with my friends before class when Sam called my name.

"Hey Yahya."

I leaned over casually with a big goofy grin. I was slick.

"Yeah?"

"Your ears are crooked."

Wow. Just like that, I went from relaxed and friendly to self-conscious and uncomfortable. My face went blood red.

"Yeah, I—I was born that way." I replied, trying to laugh it off. Really? I was born that way? Was that the best I could do? As soon as the teacher entered the room, I asked to use the bathroom. I speed-walked there and when I looked in the bathroom mirror, I was crying. I looked at my ears. My ears had never seemed so goofy and ugly in my life.

For those of you who haven't seen me in person, yeah, my ears are folded. They stick out a bit and look like radars. I can hear perfectly fine, and there's really nothing wrong with them. But Sam had labeled me as different, and now I *felt* very, very different.

A couple years earlier, when I was 12, my father asked me if I wanted cosmetic surgery to make my ears look "normal." We went to the hospital to learn about the surgery, but I was denied because my hearing was healthy. I don't blame my dad for making me feel self-conscious. He saw my difference and thought he could help me feel better about myself with the surgery. Looking back, though, my dad's comments really set me up to fall apart when Sam gave me her "helpful" feedback.

Anyhow, I went to the nurse and went home early. I cried myself to sleep that night and the next morning, I looked at myself in the mirror. Do you know what I realized?

My ears weren't that bad after all. I even kind of liked them. They were part of what made me, me. Here is what I've learned from that experience, and from my work:

#1 If you don't define yourself, others will define you.

Imagine someone calls you a snob. You wouldn't like that, right? Well, if you aren't certain of who you really are, it becomes easy to believe what others say about you. Without a clear sense of yourself, you'll end up believing what everyone says you are.

Now, if someone you care about makes an observation about you, then listen. If someone who loves you tells you it's important for you to lose weight and stay healthy, it might be worth listening to. But if someone you don't care about calls you fat, and you aren't already comfortable with your own image, you may end up believing you're fat.

#2 It's one thing to have a label; it's another thing to let it control your life.

Look, everyone has a label—or several labels. They can't be avoided. Other people give them to us and we give them to ourselves. The important difference is whether you choose to accept those labels or not. You can't control what other people say about you, but you can control how it affects you.

Say someone calls you dumb. You can't stop people from saying it, but you can choose whether to believe it or not. It's a big difference.

#3 Every label sticks until you peel it off.

Unfortunately, labels don't fall off just because time passes. If you can't get past what others say about you, you'll believe what they say not only now, but also in the future. Many adults still carry the labels they accepted at a young age. Get to know yourself and those labels fall right off!

The moment you judge a person, you lose your power to positively influence or inspire them.

Don't forget—we don't just receive labels; we give them. It can be tempting to fall in with the crowd and slap those labels on someone who appears different. But when you label someone, you stop seeing him or her for who they truly are.

This is especially important for people who are tagged as "bad kids" and "troublemakers." I work with many young people who have made some bad choices, but if I judged them as "no good" or "hopeless," then I'd never truly be able to see them or help them.

The ironic thing is that we think we understand a person better by labeling, but actually, labels blind us to a person's true self.

MoMENT oF CHALLENGE

Think about a person you have labeled. Maybe you think they're the nerd, the class clown or the shy kid. Find something you have in common (even if it's a class) and talk to them. You may learn they have more sides to their personality than you gave them credit for. Don't worry about what other people think. Be your own person.

People are complex and full of contradictions. There are football players who watch chick flicks, Honor Roll students who like death metal and skaters who read Shakespeare. Labeling a person eliminates all the cool quirks in his or her personality. Don't take the fun out of being human by giving labels, and don't take the fun out of being yourself by believing what others say about you.

And last of all; don't let labels kill your potential. Did you know Albert Einstein couldn't speak until age four, or read until age seven? Isaac Newton was a terrible student, Winston Churchill failed the 6th grade and Thomas Edison's teachers told him he was too stupid to learn anything. Can you imagine what our world would be like if these geniuses had bought into their labels? Take a step back and remember that the words we use on other people can shape their futures. But the words that we use on ourselves have the ultimate power, so choose your words carefully. And if the words used on you have been chosen carelessly, *don't* let them dictate *your* future.

Life Lesson #5

It's not what you hear with your ears, it's what goes on between your ears that defines who you are as a person.

Discussion Questions

1) Explain how words can lift someone up.

2) Explain how words can hurt someone permanently.

3) You will believe what others say about you unless you have a strong _____ _____ _____.

4) Since you can't control what other people say about you, what can you control?

   _____

   _____

5) Have you ever "labeled" someone or yourself before?
   a. If so, why?

   _____

   _____

6) Agree or Disagree: "You should never believe anything other people say about you." Discuss.

   _____

   _____

   _____

   _____

CHAPTER 6
Friends
The Good, the Bad, the Ugly

"A friend to all is a friend to none."

—*Aristotle*

If you think your 493 friends on Facebook or Twitter are all really your friends, you might need to reevaluate your definition of "friend." A friend is someone you're close with and is there for you throughout the good times and bad times. A friend is someone you know you can always go out and have a good time with. Friends are select, and valuable.

But friends can also cause us stress and trouble. Sometimes, the people we think are friends turn out not to be. Sometimes, friendships force us to make hard choices. Sometimes, telling the difference between our friends and our enemies is almost impossible.

This chapter won't teach you how to make a hundred new friends. It won't suddenly make you super popular. It will talk about what exactly a friend is, why they're so important in our lives and how you can tell if your friend is really your friend. It might even help you be a better friend to someone, and what could be better than that?

What are Friends?

In some ways, our friends can be even more important in our lives than our families. After all, we *choose* our friends, so they're a better reflection of who we are than the family we're born into, which we have no control over. And yet, most people don't think about what friends really are, or how we make them. They just appear in our lives. But here are some reasons a stranger becomes a friend:

- **Common interests**

Maybe you both like hockey, and started talking about it one day. Maybe one day, you both discover you love Justin Beiber, Drake, Selena Gomez, Kid Cudi or some other artist. Maybe you both love horror movies. In these cases, you instantly begin your friendship with something to share.

- **Chemistry**

You might think that shy people always make friends with shy people, or loud ones with loud. This isn't always true, though. Sometimes, people with similar personalities make poor friends, and it takes a strange pair to make a great match. You know, opposites attract. You can tell your science teacher I said that!

- **Shared Adventure**

One day, you may go through a tough experience with someone you hardly know. It happens in movies all the time! Afterwards, you may be closer to that person. Overcoming challenges can help people cut through the baloney and reveal their true character.

- **A Third Party**

Maybe you are friends with someone else who introduces you to another friend. This can lead to big groups of friends who all hang out together.

When we look at where our friends come from, we can understand ourselves a little better. For example, if you are naturally shy and introverted, maybe you make your friends through other friends, because you don't go up to people on your own. Maybe your friends are outgoing and loud, because you tend to be the quiet, thoughtful one. In any case, the better you understand your friends, the better you understand yourself.

Friends vs. Acquaintances

Friends are awesome! You chill with them, hang with them, share secrets with them, go on adventures with them and watch their backs while they watch yours. Friends are fun multipliers—almost anything is more fun with friends! Going to the movies: alone or with friends? Amusement parks? Eating out? Think back on some of your favorite memories, and I'll bet a lot of them have friends in the picture. In your life, you probably have a few close friends. I used the words "few close friends" because maybe you have two or three, or maybe you have 10 or 20, but the number probably falls in that range. If you don't have any friends, don't sweat it. This chapter will help you.

An acquaintance, well, that's just a person you know. Maybe you sit next to that person in Biology lab and you've had a couple of laughs. Maybe you played in band together and shared a music stand. Acquaintances are fine, and sometimes they become friends, but they're not the same as friends. You wouldn't tell them your fears or struggles, you wouldn't trust them with truly important issues and you usually wouldn't open up to them beyond the superficial "Hey-how-are-you."

Why is this distinction important? Nowadays, technology has made it easier to do almost everything—including make friends. Long ago, in the ancient times before computers and smartphones, when dinosaurs roamed the earth, people had to make friends by talking to and meeting other people. If you wanted to reconnect with a long-lost friend, you had to call them on the phone, if you could find their phone number. Then came social networking—sites like MySpace, Friendster and Facebook.

Facebook changed the way we relate to people in the 21st century. It lets us search for that long-lost friend by just typing the name in the search bar. And you can chat right there on the site, too. In many ways, these are great innovations that have helped bring people together.

But in other ways, Facebook has watered down the meaning of the word "friend." Now, anyone can be your "friend" as long as they accept your "friend request." Many people consider a large number of Facebook friends to be a sign of prestige or status. Some people send out friend requests to people they don't even know in hopes of appearing more popular. With Facebook, you can be "friends" with your cousin's neighbor's older brother in college whom you never met but is apparently really cool.

Don't get me wrong—sites like Facebook have done a lot to bring people together. And feeling connected is a great feeling.

But how connected are you, really?

If you have a Facebook or other social network account, think of how many friends you have. Can you name them all? Can you name half of them? How many of them would you tell a secret to, or trust with something important?

Now, I'm not saying to de-friend your Facebook friends or shut down your account. You are probably already aware that a friend on Facebook is not the same thing as a real friend. What I'm saying is that you need to always keep the difference clear in your own mind. Having a thousand online friends doesn't necessarily make you cooler, friendlier or more popular. It just means you sent out a lot of requests and a lot of people clicked the "confirm" button. Keep it in perspective.

All of this leads me to a bigger, more important point about friends, which is:

Quality vs. Quantity.

Would you rather have 50 beaten-up, scuffed-up shoes, or one brand new pair of shoes that were built to last? Would you rather have 20 pairs of dirty socks, or one amazing leather jacket? Would you rather watch 10 bad movies or one great one? The answer is easy. Unfortunately, with people, it's a trickier question.

When it comes to your friends (real, flesh-and-blood ones), you have to think about the *quality* of friends versus the *quantity*. Would you rather have 50 people who *appear* to be friends or one real, true friend? If you go out and try to get as many friends as possible, those friends won't be worth much. The first time you look to one of them for advice, or need a favor, they won't be able to help you. But the one real friend will be there in a heartbeat if you ever need him or her. One real friendship may not put you in the ranks of the "popular" crowd, but that's a whole different animal.

When I was in school, I wanted to be really popular. I hung out with one of the popular kids to try and fit in, and he led me to make some pretty poor choices. We would stay out until 2 a.m. shooting cars and houses with paintball guns. In the winter, we'd pelt moving cars with snowballs. I thought it would be a lot of fun, but all I got out of these dangerous, stupid stunts was the thought that I was fitting in with the cool crowd. My actions weren't my "friend's" fault; he made his choices and I made mine. Since I didn't know who I was, and thought it was important to be popular, I made some poor choices. My father tried to guide me, but at that time, I thought I was smarter, cooler and better than him. Turns out that we're both humans who sometimes make mistakes.

As you'll learn next chapter, my father and I have not always seen eye-to-eye. And when you're 16, and think you're cool like I did, advice from parents is hard to take. He said to me: "Your friends will change. In five or 10 years, you probably won't have the same friends you do today. So you had better know yourself well." Of course, I did NOT want to hear his advice when he gave it. It took me many years to see his wisdom. But he was right. If you don't understand yourself, you won't know the true friends from the false ones, and you could end up making some foolish decisions. If you're wondering how my relationship with my father is now, well let's just say that we're both able to love openly, forgive quickly and enjoy each other's time. In other words, we're like best friends now.

Believe it or not, I have *fewer* friends today than I did when I was 16, but you know what? As I'm writing this book now at the age of 23, I have to say that the friends I have today are better for me and mean much more to me. These friends help me grow as a human being, challenge me to see different perspectives, encourage me to be honest and give from my heart. The best part is that they take full responsibility for their mistakes and shortcomings. They don't just talk your ear off and complain about their own and other people's problems while playing the blame game. That can be extremely toxic and draining to your growth. Make sure you filter the energy drainers out and allow the honest and responsible friends in. I wouldn't trade them for anything. See? Quality over quantity.

Real vs. False Friends

Okay, we keep talking about "true friends" and "false friends," but how can you tell the difference? Good question. Figuring this out takes thinking, imagining and asking yourself some really tough questions.

And one last thing to remember—just because someone isn't a true friend does not make them a bad person. It just means you aren't really that close, and you should be cautious about letting them lead you into possibly destructive choices. Friends have influence. Let them influence you towards a positive direction.

TRUE FRIENDS: Won't pressure you to do negative things.

FALSE FRIENDS: May pressure you into doing things you know are wrong.

TRUE FRIENDS: Accept you for who you are.

FALSE FRIENDS: Will try to push you to become someone you're not.

TRUE FRIENDS: Want the best for you.

FALSE FRIENDS: Want the best for themselves.

TRUE FRIENDS: Will take time to listen to you and your feelings.

FALSE FRIENDS: Don't want to hear that emo stuff.

TRUE FRIENDS: Can be trusted with a secret.

FALSE FRIENDS: Cannot be trusted to keep a secret.

TRUE FRIENDS: Will tell you the ugly truth, even when it hurts.

FALSE FRIENDS: Won't say what needs to be said, or will only flatter you.

TRUE FRIENDS: Will go through thick and thin with you.

FALSE FRIENDS: Will only go through easy stuff with you.

And here's the ironic part: it may look like the people with lots of friends and attention are the happiest, but if you don't also have at least one solid, deep, true friend, you'll actually feel really alone.

MoMENT oF CHALLENGE

Think of people you consider friends. Then for each one, go through the categories above and see which ones they fall into. It probably won't be all one or the other, but it's good to be aware.

Saying Adios to the Ugly

Then there's the sucky part of friendship—moving on. I'm sure you've learned already that people you were friends with before aren't always your friends now. Well, some of your friends now won't be your friends in a couple of years, either. I'm sure you're wondering how to prevent this.

You can't.

Our friends are our friends based on who we are in the moment. At one time, you might have certain interests and needs that your friends fill for you. Those needs change. YOU change. Other people change. What was once a perfect matchup of personalities just doesn't work anymore.

And that's okay.

It's *natural* to outgrow your friends. If you keep all the same friends your entire life, you aren't growing (and neither are your friends). Growing and changing open you up to new possibilities, but they can also cause you to leave behind old familiar things (and people). And that's okay.

What's not okay is letting that turn into drama. When people outgrow a friendship, they should be able to move forward maturely, but it isn't always that tidy. People start name-calling, rumor spreading, and trash talking if they feel like they've been "friend-dumped." What's really happening, though, is that as you mature and grow as a person, it makes other people uncomfortable. The people you grow up with are used to who you were in the past. Now that you're changing and moving forward, they have to face themselves and their own self-perception. This can be scary and uncomfortable. But remember—if someone has a problem with you growing up and changing, don't make it your problem, too. Avoid negativity and drama. Just pick up and move on.

So how do you know if your friendships are good for you or not? Well, the way I see it, your friends do one of two things to you:

1. Lift you up.
2. Drag you down.

It really is that simple. If the people in your life lift you up, then great, it sounds like the foundation for a healthy and dynamic friendship. If there are people in your life who drag you down, then let them go. Saying goodbye doesn't have to look like an episode of *Real Housewives* or a scene from *Fight Club*. You can just let the friendship fade away easily. Don't be mean or cold; just move forward.

And remember, too—some people don't WANT to be lifted up. They are afraid of living life on a new level. These are the kinds of people you'll outgrow, and that's okay.

Okay, So Now What?

So, you know it's important to tell the difference between your friends and your acquaintances, between actual friends and online "friends" and between true friends and false ones. But now comes the money question: how do you MAKE the true friends? "Yahya," you're asking, "are you going to give us some complicated plan with lots of rules and guidelines? How hard are you gonna make this?"

Relax. There's just one rule.

To make good friends, you have to BE a good friend.

You've probably heard that one before. It's kind of a cliché, but it's still true. If you aren't happy with your relationships with other people, they won't magically change without you changing first. Do the things that good friends do—listen, speak with honesty, accept—then your true friends will show themselves.

Your relationships with them will get stronger. You will understand one another in new ways, and understand yourself better, as well. You will have someone to guide you into the future, and whether this friend is someone you've known for many years or someone new in your life, a true friend will help you become the best you, that you can be. That's the true gift of friendship.

Relationships

For some of you, romantic relationships are something you aren't concerned with yet, something you want to leave to the future. That's fine. But for many of you, your boyfriend or girlfriend is a major part of your life. Relationships can be a real source of strength and inspiration, but they can also cause a lot of stress. But every relationship is an opportunity for you to learn more about yourself and about others.

I've had a pretty steady relationship for much of my life. My girlfriend, Kate, and I have been together since I was 15 and she was 14. Yeah, high school sweethearts and prom king and queen. I'm a much different man than I was then, and she's a different woman. We've had ups and downs. We've changed a lot. What we've learned is that change is a necessary part of life. It's not fair and not realistic to expect you or your partner to never change. You may change and grow together, or you may change and grow apart. What is important is that you are aware of these changes and respect them, and respect one another.

In my own experience—both with being in relationships and with helping other people in theirs—I've learned that romantic relationships come down to three basic types:

1. **Physical:** This is the "he/she is so hot I want to be with him/her so bad he/she is soooo sexy." It might be the starting point for some relationships, but isn't a strong foundation for a long and healthy one. No one stays pretty or hot forever.

2. **Fairy Tale Romance:** This is based all on stories, movies and unrealistic expectations. No one's relationship has a "happily ever after" in it. There's always more work to do, always more bumps in the road ahead. People who get in a relationship and expect a prince or princess to fulfill all their dreams will soon get a cold bucket of reality dumped on them.

3. **Friendship:** This is not a "let's-just-be-friends" relationship. This is a romantic relationship in which your partner is also one of your best friends. You can confide in each other and trust each other with secrets. In my opinion, all strong romantic relationships need to be a lot like strong friendships; otherwise your interest in the other person (as well as your patience for their shortcomings) will fade.

All You Need is L.O.V.E.

I am not about to give you a long list of rules for having successful relationships. I like to keep things simple. For me, the most important rule is this:

_L.O.V.E._ no matter what the challenge maybe be.

That stands for **_Listening Overcomes Virtually Everything_**. A huge weakness in many relationships is the inability to listen. People want to be listened to, but don't take the time to actually listen.

If you actually listen to your partner—and not just wait for them to stop talking so you can talk—you'll understand their needs, their fears and where they are coming from. Problems in the relationship are easier to solve when you understand each other. So the next time you're discussing (arguing about) something with your partner, stop trying so hard to get your point across. Shut your mouth, open your ears and listen to what he or she has to say. Understand this principle, and I promise you something great will come out of it.

Life Lesson #6

There are two types of people in your life. People who tear you down or build you up. If people are trying to tear you down, that only means that you are above them. Don't stoop down to their level; build them up with you.

Discussion Questions

1) **Describe the characteristics of a true friend.**

2) **What are some ways to meet friends listed in the chapter?**

a. Why is it important to understand <u>how</u> you make friends?

_____

_____

3) Think of one of your best friends.

a. How did you first meet?

_____

_____

b. How has your friendship changed over time?

_____

_____

c. What qualities make that person a good friend?

_____

_____

4) Think about all of your friends as a group.

a. What characteristics do they have in common?

_____

_____

b. What do you think this says about you as a person?

_____

_____

5) What happened to Yahya when he was caught in an unhealthy friendship?

_____

_____

a. Have you ever been caught in an unhealthy friendship? Describe what happened.

_____

_____

6) What is the difference between friends and acquaintances?

_____

_____

7) Approximately how many online friends do you have?

_____

_____

   a. Do you think this is too many? Acceptable? Not enough?

_____

_____

   b. How are online friends different from in-person friends?

_____

_____

8) Agree or Disagree: "Being popular is a bad thing." Discuss.

_____

_____

_____

_____

CHAPTER 7

Family

The World is Your Family

> *"The bond that links your true family is not one of blood, but of respect and joy in each other's life."*
>
> —*Richard Bach*

O f all the chapters in this book, the chapter on family might be the most personal, most challenging and most rewarding for me. I love my family dearly, but it's taken me a long time and a lot of work to build healthy relationships, and I'm still in the process of building. It's taken me years to define exactly what my family is and what it means to me. That definition has changed over time and will probably continue to change. But hey—I have nothing to hide from you, and I want to share my personal story of my family life to show you how you, too, might be able to build a positive relationship with your family or caretakers, no matter how many problems you've had in the past. Blaming your problems on the hand that life has dealt you will only waste energy and won't make you any happier. So here goes.

My Story, Part I

I was born in Makkah, Saudi Arabia, but moved to the United States when I was five years old. My parents divorced when I was just a baby, and I never knew my real mother. My father remarried an Iraqi woman, and I've always called her "mom." She is such a great person. They both are really great people.

Looking back, I think my father was struggling to find his own identity. He was married several different times, and focused most of his attention on his own interests. When I was little and needed his love and approval, he seemed distant and uninterested, or maybe he was going through his own struggles and couldn't give me his attention. I'm still not sure. As a result, we had a rocky relationship for many years.

Things got bad when I turned 13 years old. My stepmom and dad decided to get a divorce and I had to choose whom I wanted to live with. Do I choose to live with my dad who is my flesh and blood, or my stepmom who raised me most of my life? I chose to live with my father. I was torn. I was hitting a major identity crisis; I didn't know who I was, who I was supposed to be, or even what I believed in. I had no direction or focus, and (as you remember from last chapter) hung around with friends who really weren't good for me, though I didn't see it that way at the time. It was a pretty confusing, angry period of my life.

I blamed my family for all of this. I resented them, and at times I hated them. I couldn't understand them and they couldn't understand me. I especially struggled with my dad. It felt so unfair.

The breaking point was one night after going out to the movies with my friends. I was really frustrated, and one of my friends offered to let me stay with him. I knew I wanted to, but had a choice to make—do I tell my dad, or just go?

I just went.

My friend and I used my new freedom to fool around and get in trouble. I knew I had to go back eventually, and after three days, I returned. I expected to be punished. I figured I'd walk inside and he'd start yelling and screaming.

Well, you can imagine my shock when I came inside and saw him calmly sitting down to dinner. He'd even set out an empty plate for me across the table. He asked me to sit and eat.

Sweet, I thought. I'm getting off easy. We ate, and afterwards, I went into the bathroom to wash up.

"Take off your glasses, please," my dad asked. (I wore prescription glasses back then). It seemed like a weird request, but I took my glasses off and set them on the sink.

Suddenly my dad's fist crashed into my face and sent me sprawling into the tub. I was out cold.

When I woke up, I saw my dad crying. I didn't hit him back or anything. I saw, right then, a side of my dad's humanity he'd never let me see before. I realized that he was just a man trying to do the best to raise his son. It was a critical moment in our relationship. This moment taught me that we all have goodness inside of us but sometimes it doesn't show immediately. That's why I do my best to be nonjudgmental when it comes to a person's behavior and actions. The moment we judge a person, we lose all our power to influence and inspire them in a better direction. Read the previous sentence again. Deep, isn't it?

To Love or Hate?

The word "family" can cause so many different reactions. For those who have supportive, functional families, with good communication and lots of love and support, family is a source of strength, power and inspiration. The rest of us look at families like this and wonder, "Why not me? Why couldn't I have that?"

For those with families that are dysfunctional (and there are a lot of us), families can create anger, division, blame and can suck away your direction, motivation and positive energy.

In my experience, I've worked with families of all types. And you know what? The vast majority of families have problems. Big ones, small ones, it doesn't matter. Out of the people I grew up with, 95% of them had reasons to be angry with their parents. They resented them, they ignored them and they even hated them. Unlike friends, who we can choose to make part of our lives, families are like a bad hand in a card game—you're stuck with them. It just seems unfair. So families, which can and should be a great source of love and positivity in our lives, are more often than not a negative force—that is, if we choose to let them be.

Values

When we say "family," most people think of mom and dad, stepparents, brothers and sisters and then the extended family. But I'm going to turn that around a little. No, a lot. *Your family doesn't have to mean your "flesh and blood."* A family has two things keeping it together—established values and established love.

When you hear "family values," it's usually from politicians. That's not how I'm using it. What I mean by family values is the system of beliefs that keeps a family together. Maybe one family believes that each important decision gets left up to dad, while another family believes that everyone should get a vote. Some families value together time, while others value each member having independence. There is no single set of values that all families share, but as long as those within the family embrace those values, the family functions together. If they don't all agree on the values, then there's tension and dysfunction.

For example, if everyone in the family agrees that stepmom should be respected and treated with the same respect that mom would get, that aspect of the family would function smoothly. However, if the kids aren't on board, and won't give stepmom the same respect, there will, without a doubt, be an argument—or many arguments—until things get straightened out.

The other thing all families need is established love. That love needs to be both shown and expressed out loud—by parents and by children. Love holds families together.

That's it. Just two things, but they're big things. So what gets in the way?

Needs.

The things that parents need from their children are appreciation and responsibility. They need the feedback from their kids that they have been great and effective parents. They need to know they did a good job taking care of you. Parents also want to know that if something were to happen to them, that you would be responsible enough to take control of your life by not getting sidetracked by the distractions around you (We'll talk more about distractions later . . . . let's not get distracted now).

What children need from parents are acceptance, support, love and approval. They need to know that their parents love them for who they are and are proud of them. In a healthy parent–child relationship, all these things are flowing back and forth. In an unhealthy one, something is missing. Someone isn't getting what he or she needs, the balance is thrown off and people become angry.

These needs must be met unconditionally, too. Many people fall into the "if" trap. "Well, maybe I'd show more appreciation to my parents IF they showed they loved me." "I want to approve of my child, and I would, IF he took more responsibility." When either the parent or the child waits for the other to start doing the right thing, the cycle of frustration and anger just keeps spinning, like a whirlpool, sucking all the happiness and positivity out of a family.

MoMENT oF CHALLENGE

Take a moment and think about your family. Who is part of it? How are your relationships with those people? Do you have people outside your family meeting your emotional needs? What can you do for your family right now to show them that they did a great job for doing their best? In other words, how can you appreciate them for all their hard work?

I'm not saying you should be an obedient slave to your parents. Sometimes parents are wrong. Sometimes you are wrong. What you need to do is understand what *your* values are. Some of them may have come from your family and others may have been discovered on your own. You can disagree with your parents and still have a loving relationship with them. Always keep a clear sense of who and what you are—your family and friends may eventually leave your life, but your core values will always be with you. In your troubles with family, never lose yourself.

Some people misunderstand the role of parents. They think, "My friends are cool, but my parents aren't. Why can't my parents be cool, too?"

Bad news. The job of a parent is NOT to be your friend. The parents who act like their kids' buddies often end up with a dysfunctional relationship. A parent's main job is to be a *role model*. Parents should be showing kids how to live a responsible, happy life. **Don't get me**

wrong, you should always feel like you can trust your parents with what you have to share. When kids become adults, then it's a little different, but when you're a teen, don't blame your parents for being tough on you and giving you boundaries (I know this might be hard to accept). If anything, they are doing their best to raise you. It's not like they were given a manual called "THE PARENT'S GUIDE TO RAISING CHILDREN" when you were born.

You may be wondering what you can do if your parents aren't meeting one or some of your emotional needs. What happens is that you'll satisfy those needs any way you can. Maybe a friend's mother will give you the love your own mother never does. Maybe an uncle can show the approval your father never gave. Maybe a gang can show you the security you always wanted. But here's the catch. Some of the things you will do to satisfy your needs are good choices, while others are bad choices. My point is you will meet those needs one way or another, whether you realize it's bad for you or not. So do your best to find people who don't want to harm others and who see the best in you. If you form relationships with people who actually care about you and want nothing but the best for you, you'll discover something incredible—your family doesn't have to be just mother-father-brother-sister-you. The whole world can be your family.

Let that sink in for a minute.

Pretty deep, huh?

Be an Example

As I mentioned before, many people blame their families for their anger and frustration with life. But as I've also mentioned before, blaming gets people nowhere. It's a waste of energy, and hurts you more than the person you blame. So here's how you can make the change.

1) **Stop the blame**

   Yes, this is much easier said than done. But the sooner you can stop laying your shortcomings at your family's feet, the sooner you can move forward and heal.

2) **Make the first move**

   Don't wait for the troublesome family member to change first. When you are first to acknowledge the problems of the past and your desire to move forward, it will begin the healing process. It also may astonish your family.

3) **Be an example**

   Do you want respect? Treat people with respect. Do you want love? Love more. It's hard, I know. Look, I've been in the same place. It's especially hard when you're in the middle of an argument. That's when you'll want to dump the whole healing process and go back to the anger. But when it's especially hard is also when it's especially important.

When you do these things, something seriously cool may happen. Not only will the "problem" family member begin to trust you and treat you more fairly, they may even be inspired by you. We think that parents are always supposed to take care of and teach their children, but the children can teach their parents, too. By being a positive example, you will lead others to live a better life.

In the end, you can't control your family. You may even give your very best effort to heal a broken relationship, and fail. Some people are totally unwilling to change. But what you CAN control is yourself and your reactions. If you feel alone because of your family's treatment, it's because you've allowed yourself to feel lonely. Build healthy relationships with people outside your family, and keep setting a positive example. Most parents really want the best for their children, even if they can't agree on what that "best" thing is. However, if you grow up and take ownership of your life and show that you take life seriously, you will get the love, appreciation and respect you deserve.

My Story, Part II

Since I was 16, I have been working on my relationship with my father, and on myself. The advice I've given in this chapter isn't stuff I've thought of. It's stuff I've lived. It took a lot of work and many years, but we have reached an understanding with each other.

My father moved to Egypt, and I recently decided to go over there and see him. While I have great relationships with my friends—who are like my family in many ways—he is still my father, and I wanted what I've always wanted from him: love.

The trip was a success. My father and I sat outside, talking for hours and he apologized for not doing a better job as a dad for me. You remember L.O.V.E. from last chapter? Well, I showed my dad lots of L.O.V.E. that important night. When I *listened* to him—truly listened—I was able to learn about his difficult childhood and his sincere feelings. During our long talk, we talked about everything. Though we still disagree on some things—okay, on almost everything—we now have a relationship based on communication and love, not on silence and resentment. It took almost a quarter century of life to develop a healthy, respectful relationship with my dad, but we have one now, and I know we'll both be better off because of it.

Many people also ask me if I've ever tried to find my real mother. I have, but with no success yet. I know only that she lives in Thailand, and someday I may travel there to find her. Once that happens, who knows? But even without her in my life, I know that I've built enough loving relationships around me that I feel satisfied. I also have four brothers and three sisters who aren't my full-blooded siblings but I love them regardless. To me, they will always be a part of my life. Since you're reading this book now, you've become part of my family. I genuinely believe that love heals all problems and all wounds.

Remember—family isn't blood; it's love and values.

Life Lesson #7

It doesn't matter whether you were abandoned, abused, neglected or confused. What matters is whether you are using your past to bring out the best in you or the worst in you. Learn from it.

Discussion Questions

1) **How does Yahya's story illustrate the idea that "the whole world can be your family"?**

   _____

   _____

2) **After the incident in the bathroom, why do you think Yahya's father cried?**

   _____

   _____

3) **What emotional needs do parents have? What emotional needs do children have?**

   _____

   _____

   a. **Think about your own family. Are everyone's needs being met in healthy ways?**

   _____

4) Explain the difference between functional and dysfunctional families?

_____

_____

5) What does "shared family values" mean?

_____

_____

   a. What are your family's shared values?

_____

_____

6) Describe the three things you can do to improve your family relationships.

7) Agree or disagree: "A family relationship is always a work in progress." Discuss.

_____

_____

_____

_____

CHAPTER 8
Feelings

Cry Me a River

"Feelings are much like waves, we can't stop them from coming but we can choose which one to surf."

—Jonatan Martensson

Everyone has them.

They pop up at the most inconvenient, unexpected times.

They are unavoidable, and can destroy relationships.

You can't see them, but you know they're there.

We can't seem to find a way to control them.

What are they?

Emotions!

Emotions are strange little things. On the one hand, they seem so uncontrollable and pointless. You can't see, hear, touch, taste or smell them. They don't make any money, they can't be bought or sold and they usually vanish soon after they appear.

On the other hand, few things rule our lives the way emotions do. In the Declaration of Independence, Thomas Jefferson declared that the pursuit of happiness is one of our basic human rights. People put great amounts of energy into finding love and friendship. People carrying fear (more on that soon) can be weighed down for years with that emotion, and people who follow their anger (more on that, too) often find themselves unhappy (or even miserable) and in deep trouble.

So what are emotions? How can these little, invisible things control our lives?

Simple. Because we let them.

I Feel Good!

So what exactly are emotions and feelings? We recognize them, but they aren't anything material, tangible or physical. You can't pick them up with your fingers or look at them under a microscope or step on them. They can't be grown, cooked, burned or squished. No, emotions are responses or reactions to events and situations that happen in our lives.

So what?

Well, just as we talked about with friends and family, if you can control the way you react to different situations, you can take ownership of your life and stop feeling like a victim. The same thing applies with feelings. If you can realize that emotions are not actual, physical objects, and that they are simply responses to events—responses that can be controlled—then you don't have to be a victim to your emotions.

"But I don't feel like a victim, Yahya," you might be saying. "They're not beating me up. They're not pushing me around."

Really?

So, when something happens and you're really sad about it, that sadness doesn't take over all of your thoughts?

Or, when someone makes you mad, you don't sometimes react in ways that you regret later?

Or, when you're really excited for something to happen, that happiness doesn't distract you from anything else in your life?

The fact is that emotions, those big and little responses to events in our lives, *become* major events in our lives. Often, in fact, the emotional reaction takes on more power than the event itself. So while emotions may not have any size or weight, they do have a lot of power.

Are Emotions Real?

Whoa! Deep question.

But it is a question worth thinking about. On the one hand, duh! Of course they're real. In our everyday experiences, we encounter the very real power of feelings. They drive the things we do and shape our goals and futures. People work very hard to find happiness and avoid pain, to seek out laughter and overcome sorrow.

On the other hand, as we said before, emotions are reactions and responses, but don't have any physical properties. And they really only exist in one place—in your head. They are little signals your brain cooks up to deal with—or get ready for— different situations.

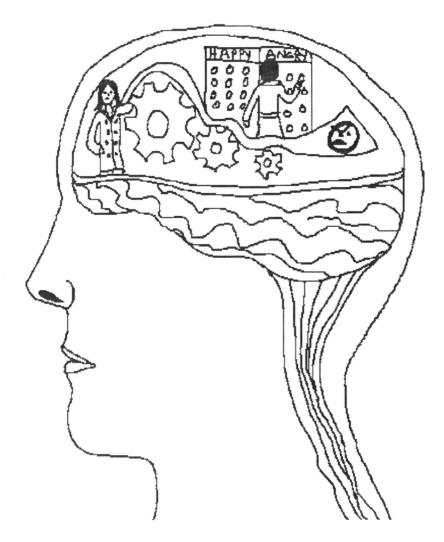

Hmm. Not so easy now. Are they real or aren't they?

Well I'm not going to give you an answer. That's for you to decide. But I *will* give you some suggestions on how you can live a healthy "emotional" life, and not be a victim to those little brain signals.

Fact: *We all have emotions.*

Seems obvious, but many people try to bottle up their emotions or ignore them. Some people don't even know how to express them and this is not a healthy way to deal with emotions. Your goal shouldn't be to stop having emotions, that would make you a zombie, and while zombies can be pretty cool, I wouldn't want to be one, and neither would you.

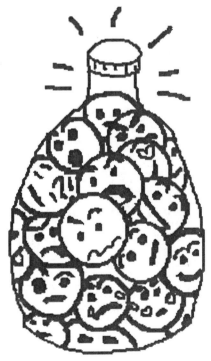

No, a better approach is to learn to recognize your emotions and control them, or even better, guide them. Martial arts taught me this. As you know, I had a lot of anger and frustration as a young man. I was angry with my dad, I was angry with my biological mom and I didn't know why. Those feelings built up inside of me and I started making bad choices because of them, as you also know, I bottled up emotions, I hid from them and I ran from them—I did anything but face them and overcome them.

Taekwondo showed me how to take those emotions and control them so my mind would be clear. You don't need to practice martial arts, but you should learn how to control your emotional responses to events. It's all about channeling that built up energy into motion. One way to do this is to play a sport that you like. Another way to express your emotions is to tap into the artistic nature inside of you. You can dance, sing, draw, sculpt, rap, play an instrument, and write poems and more.

But how can you control your emotions? The same way you control fear—recognize them.

Sounds simple, but it takes a lifetime of work to achieve, and most people never even try. Some people hide and ignore their emotions until they explode at exactly the wrong time. Other people are attached to their emotions and believe they make them who they are—even the negative ones, *especially* the negative ones. Angry people stay angry because they believe their anger makes them who they are. They are so attached to their feelings that it's like an addiction. Maybe you know someone who's always mad. They'll keep putting themselves in situations to get mad because of that rush and sense of power they get.

Even the language we use makes us think this way. If someone steals your phone, you say, "I am angry," as though anger is who you are. But you aren't anger. You are you, and anger is just the emotion you're feeling. Really, a better way to express it would be "I'm feeling anger" or "I am experiencing angry feelings now." It's a little more complex to say, but more accurate.

Think of emotions like the hiccups. You get the hiccups, but you don't think of yourself as a "hiccups person." It just happens, and when you wait a little while, they go away. If you recognize that your emotions are not who you are, but are natural responses to events, they'll lose their power to rule your life. They'll arrive, you'll recognize them and then they'll pass. You'll be free of the prison of strong feelings, and you'll advance beyond 99% of the rest of the human population.

Crazy, right?

So far, I've been ragging on feelings pretty hard. But they can also be incredibly helpful to you. You see if you learn what events make you feel a certain way, emotions can serve as guidelines for you. If you realize that you seem to get angry every time you're late for something, recognize that. Stop being late and you'll stop getting mad.

MoMENT oF CHALLENGE

Next time you feel angry, take a step back. Breathe. Imagine you aren't angry, but you have the hiccups. Keep breathing. Don't act on the anger. Just see what happens.

One trap people fall into is trying to experience only "good" emotions and never "bad" ones. I remember one particular event in my life that taught me about this. I was working as a dental assistant, and a patient came in and *asked* the doctor to perform root canals on all of his teeth. A root canal is a surgical procedure in which a chunk of nerve is taken out of your tooth. Most people hate them. Getting ONE root canal can make a person miserable. So of course, the dentist asked the man why he would want that. The patient replied that he didn't want to feel pain with his teeth for the rest of his life.

Most people think of pain as "bad." But pain isn't bad. It can teach us and guide us. It tells us we're still alive. Don't try to get rid of things like pain or sadness. Acknowledge them. Realize that they happen. Learn from them.

For some reason, we treat feelings like they're something we're born knowing how to deal with. We're not. Handling your emotions isn't like eating or breathing; it is a skill, just like learning to drive a car or play an instrument. You are who you are, but you can always learn new skills. Practice the skill of managing your emotions. Don't bottle them, don't hate them and don't think they define who you are. Go on, express your emotions; be open about them and learn from experiences. Emotions are your guide but not your master.

Life Lesson #8

Emotion is a science. E-Motion: Energy in Motion. If you don't know how to guide your energy, the emotion has more control over you than you think. Acknowledge, allow and appreciate your emotions for helping you.

Discussion Questions

1) **Explain how emotions are both real and not real. Which do you think they are?**

_____

_____

2) In what ways are some people prisoners of their emotions?

_____

_____

3) List three UNHEALTHY ways people deal with emotions.

4) Explain the difference between "I am angry" and "I am feeling anger right now."

5) What are some ways to control your emotions?

_____

_____

6) How can you express yourself in a healthy way without damaging your feelings or those around you?

_____

_____

7) Agree or Disagree: "There are some emotions we should try to avoid." Discuss.

_____

_____

_____

_____

CHAPTER 9

Fear

False Expectations
Appearing Real

""Don't let the fear of striking out hold you back."

—Babe Ruth

I was in 5th grade, 11 years old, and I was walking home from school when three, big high school kids called me over from across the street.

"Hey kid!" one of them shouted. He crossed over to my side. "Give me your money."

I told him I didn't have any. All I had was my Power Rangers lunch box. The leader of the group laughed.

"No, really. Hand over your money."

His hand tapped the metal buckle on his belt. I laughed. I replied again that I didn't have any money. The kid took off his belt and hit me so hard on the left side of my face that it knocked me out. All I remember was a woman waking me up asking me if I was okay. I looked around and saw my lunchbox to my left and felt this burning pain on the side of my face. "Do you live nearby?" she asked. I told her that I lived about six blocks down. She took me to my house and I rang the doorbell. My father came down and saw my face. I was in shock the whole time until I saw him. That's when I started crying. I was hoping that no one would find out. Deep down inside, I knew that if something like that happened again, I wouldn't be able to defend myself.

I was afraid.

Fear is all around us. Some of us live with fear every single day. There are thousands of students who skip school because of the fear of being bullied. I know how that feels and it's not right. On that frightening school day all those years ago, I started a valuable journey that taught me about what fear is, how dangerous it can be and what a powerful tool it can be. It can be a gift when used correctly.

Where Fear is Born: Three Principles

Fear is as old as human beings and we actually need it. Ancient cavemen were afraid for some very good reasons. If you weren't afraid of the growling saber-toothed tiger, you might have end up as a prehistoric Pounce treat. Fear directs us to react to danger, so we can protect ourselves.

But saber-toothed tigers no longer exist; in fact, there aren't nearly as many things that threaten our lives as there were tens of thousands of years ago, and that's definitely a plus. But fear hasn't gone away. Instead of facing mortal dangers, now our brain latches onto other "threats" out there. Some of these threats are real, but most of them are imagined. All fears have some things in common:

1) We use fear to protect us from loss.

Loss of what?

Almost anything.

In ancient times, it was fear of losing our lives, our food, our loved ones or community.

Now, we fear losing a game, a chance at getting into a good college, a boyfriend or girlfriend or even comfort. Adults have fear too; fear of losing a job, a child, a family member or their homes. Think about it. What is something you are/were afraid of? Can you trace it back to fear of losing something? I bet you can.

We believe that if we are afraid, then we have a better chance of being safe. Better to see it coming than to be blindsided, right? Fear is the alarm that we use to soften the shock of losing something valuable that we love. Which brings me to . . .

2) Fear is love's shadow

Fear and love are very closely connected. We love things that are dear to us and we fear losing those things. For example, if you have someone special in your life (say, a boyfriend or girlfriend), you feel love for him or her because they bring something special and valuable to your life and make you happy. If that relationship begins to go bad, you may feel fear because you are worried about losing that person and the joy that they bring. Fear is like love's shadow—it isn't the same thing as love, but it has the same shape as love and it exists because of love.

A while ago, before I was in the career I'm in now, I was working in a chiropractor's office. A 16-year-old guy asked me a tough question. He asked me, "Is it better to be feared or to be loved?" Being feared can be valuable. For example, in a leadership position, being feared can get a lot done. By using fear you can control a person by scaring them and forcing them to do what you want them to do. I thought about it and replied that it was better to be loved. Love is the positive aspect and fear is the negative. You don't want to be the shadow; you want to be the real thing.

So we think fear protects us from danger, but it really doesn't. This brings me to my next point, which happens to be something I learned from a hypnotist:

3) Fear stands for **F**alse **E**xpectations **A**ppearing **R**eal.
   Whoa. Sounds heavy.

Fear is both real and not real at the same time. Fear is real because it has actual effects on our minds and bodies. It isn't real because it only exists in our minds. It is the perception that we might lose something, but that's it. This piece of wisdom from the hypnotist is saying that we imagine something happening (good or bad), but then we believe that those imaginary things are real.

Let me give you another example. Imagine you are struggling in one of your classes. Next week is the midterm, and you don't think you'll be ready for it. Fear creeps in. You begin convincing yourself you'll fail the class, and maybe the grade. All your friends will advance, but you'll be stuck repeating next year. Forget getting into a good college; now you're worried about just graduating. Your week is ruined, you lose sleep and everyone around you sees you falling apart.

Then, next week you take the test. You pass. Crisis averted.

Do you feel foolish?

See, the failure and disaster was all in your mind—your "false events"—but they certainly felt real to you. This is what I mean that even though fear isn't actually real, when we believe it's real, it can throw our lives out of whack and cause us to make some bad decisions.

MoMENT oF CHALLENGE

Think of a time you were afraid. What was your fear? What were you in danger of losing? What was the outcome? Did that fear help you or harm you in that moment? Now picture yourself facing that fear with courage. "All you need is 20 seconds of insane courage. Just think about that. 20 seconds of embarrassing bravery and something great will come of it. I promise." I got that from, *We Bought A Zoo.* Good movie. Watch it.

Fear: The Monster Under our Bed and In our Head

No one wants to be afraid, of course. Fear can affect us negatively in many ways.

Physically, fear can cause stress that raises our blood pressure, causes headaches, makes us lose sleep and soaks up our strength. I'm not talking about the sharp, immediate fear you feel near danger. That fear protects you. I'm talking about the long-lasting fear that eats away at us; that makes us worry and wears us down.

But mentally, it's even more damaging. Fear can cause us to make disastrous decisions based on something in our minds, not something actual and real. For example, if you are afraid of being alone or lonely, you may be desperate to find someone to date. When you're with that person, even if he or she is a bad match, you'll do anything to stay together. In the worst cases, it will be an abusive relationship, and though the sensible thing to do would be to end the relationship, you might be so much more afraid of the uncertainty and loneliness of being single that you'll stay with that person. Obviously, this is a scary situation, but fear is a powerful force that can push us to make bad choices.

Fear can also block us from taking action. Let's say you have to speak in front of an audience or have a project you need to create but you are afraid. You need to find the courage inside of you to face the fear or else you will never grow in that area of your life. Same idea goes for creating your future. You need to dream of that ideal future, and then take action to make it happen. Your future is yours to shape, but fear is one of the most powerful forces that can stop us from making it happen. What are people afraid of?

Failure.

It really makes no sense—you want to achieve a goal, but are afraid of failing at it, and so you never try. It seems ridiculous to not even try—and guarantee failure—than to risk failing. Yet that's how millions of people think.

Here is my challenge for you—don't let fear stop you from taking the actions you need to live a happy life. Fear is just a word. It's in your head. Don't let it stop you from seeing who you truly are.

That being said, the way to overcome fear isn't just to ignore it or overpower it. A lot of people may tell you to "defeat fear" or "kick fears butt" or something silly like that. I'll tell you what's a whole lot easier, identify it.

What do I mean? Take our earlier example about the midterm. You don't need to do any mental pushups or "toughen up" to deal with the fear of failing the test. But when you identify that your fear is just that—fear, and not reality—you'll find the fear is just a harmless shadow.

Also, fear doesn't always need to be overcome. In some cases, you can use fear to your advantage. When you run from fear, or try and ignore it, it will only become more powerful. However, if you embrace it, accept it and realize what it is, it can motivate you to be an even better person.

To show you what I mean, let me finish the story about the bullies I faced in 5th grade. After I'd been attacked, fear ruled me. I had no idea if I'd be attacked again. The fear haunted me like a ghost. So my father signed me up for Taekwondo.

Taekwondo is a Korean martial art. Like any martial art, you learn about kicking, punching and defending, but the mental training is the true gift. In the four years I studied Taekwondo, I learned to embrace and see through my fear. Within two years of training, I became a Junior Olympic National Champion, and I overcame my fear of being attacked. I could've let that fear rule my life, but I had dreams that I wanted to achieve. You can do the same.

Life Lesson #9

Fear is what you make of it. Don't make it anything more or anything less. Fear is sometimes a burden, but it can also be a gift when listened to carefully. Be intuitive and figure out whether or not you're being overly dramatic.

Discussion Questions

1) Fear is a way for our minds to protect us from
   _____.

   a. Give three examples of how this works.

2) Explain how fear and love are connected.

3) How is fear real? How is it not real?

   _____

   _____

4) What are some of the damaging effects of fear?

   _____

   _____

5) Explain how Yahya's story of dealing with fear made him stronger in the end.

6) Agree or disagree: "You must beat your fear in order to be free from it." Discuss.

   _____

   _____

   _____

   _____

Chapter 10

Fighting

The Peaceful Warrior

> "Nonviolence means avoiding not only external physical violence but also internal violence of spirit. You not only refuse to shoot a man, but you refuse to hate him."
>
> —Martin Luther King, Jr.

L ast chapter had a happy ending, right? I had been a victim of bullying, living a life of fear and weakness, until I found a way to overcome that fear and become a strong young man and a champion. I wasn't afraid anymore, and I wasn't going to let myself be a victim. I was a warrior. Cool ending, right?

Except it's not the ending.

Taekwondo, it turned out, was not the ultimate solution to my problems. Looking back, it was an important stepping-stone for me to become who I am today.

Who am I? Well, I like to call myself a peaceful warrior but some people call me a hippie. Either way it's all good. With that said, if you're interested in mastering power, pay close attention to what I'm about to share with you.

Fear and Fighting

Fear and fighting are closely connected. Think of almost any fighting situation, and fear is involved. In some cases, the fighting happens because of fear and in others, the fighting happens in order to create more fear.

For starters, look at bullying. Obviously, bullying is meant to create fear in the victim. The bully wants to feel more powerful, so he or she will intimidate the victim until he or she feels in control. But bullies often feel a lot of fear, too. Maybe someone else bullies them. Maybe they are afraid of appearing weak, so they pick on others to mask that. Have you ever heard of the saying that, "hurt people, hurt people." I believe there is so much truth in those words.

Speaking of hurting people, if you consider other types of fights, fear is usually at the center of them as well. What about two football players in the locker room who slug it out over a fumble that cost them the game? Maybe one is afraid of being perceived as a weak leader or is afraid of losing, while the other is afraid of being perceived as a worthless teammate. What about two girls in an argument over a guy? Maybe they are afraid of losing the boy, or are afraid of being seen as a pushover by other girls. Fights among couples are as complicated as the relationships themselves. Fear of losing one another, fear of being taken advantage of, fear of losing love, fear of being depended upon too much or not enough—the causes are endless. In nearly every instance of fighting, you can probably identify some fear that started it.

Fighting isn't always the effect of fear. Sometimes it is the cause. This is especially the case in bullying, where the bully tries to create a feeling of constant fear in the victim. But even in evenly matched fights, the message of "don't mess with me or you'll get it worse next time" usually comes through. Any way you look at it, fighting, bullying and fear are all connected.

Bullying vs. Fighting

We've talked about bullying and fighting as though they're basically the same, but I want to take a moment and draw a line between them. Bullying is one-sided. You've got someone stronger (or a group of people who feel stronger when they're together) versus someone weaker (or a group that is perceived as weaker). There's a bully and a victim, and the bully's goal is to prove his or her dominance over the victim. The victim's goal is to just get by with as little damage as possible. I believe that bullies and victims behave the way that they do for two reasons:

1. To protect themselves
2. To be validated by their peers

If you're ever in a bullying situation, reach out and ask for help. Reaching out doesn't mean you're weak, it means that you are smarter than you think.

A real fight has two sides struggling for the upper hand. It may not be evenly matched, but both sides are standing up for themselves, trying to prove they're stronger or tougher. There is no bully or victim.

The reason this matters is that most people who get into fights choose to be in them. They challenge someone or accept someone's challenge, but both sides must agree to participate. On the other hand, with bullying, victims appear to have no choice in the matter. They didn't ask to be bullied. While there is ALWAYS a choice to be a victim or not, bullying victims often cannot see other alternatives. There just doesn't seem to be many ways to overcome bullying. One of the few ways is through fighting. That's what I did.

My Story, Part III

I was a Junior Olympic Champion. I could kick, punch, leap, block and best of all, I was no longer afraid of bullies. No one messes with a black belt in Taekwondo! I was strong; I had power, both physical and mental. What a rush! My warrior's attitude started going beyond the Taekwondo mats. After I learned my skills, I wanted people to KNOW I was tough, to KNOW what a fighter I was. I would step in and defend people in situations where I wasn't even involved in the first place.

Then one day the principal took me into his office. He informed me that I was considered a weapon because of my previous experience in Taekwondo. He was joking, right?

No. He said that my black belt made me—my body—a lethal weapon.

At first I thought that was pretty cool. Me—a deadly weapon! It gave me an even bigger thrill, and boosted my ego. But as time went on, I really took his words seriously. I read more, and learned more about fighting, and thought about it a lot. Little did I know that that conversation, at the height of my power, would set me on a path that would lead to an even clearer understanding of myself.

I gave up Taekwondo a few years later. The reason, really, was that I just didn't need it anymore. You see, ever since my talk with the principal, I'd come to understand that becoming a great fighter was not my end goal, but a step along the path towards discovering who I truly am.

Who am I now?

A peaceful warrior.

I've learned a lot—a lot from being a bullying victim, a lot from being a fighter and a lot since then. One thing I've learned is that many of the world's greatest fighters are nonviolent. Mahatma Gandhi, Martin Luther King, Jr., Nelson Mandela and many more have realized that being stronger and tougher on the outside isn't always going to make you the winner. A peaceful warrior can defeat a violent one. Gandhi, King and Mandela all achieved triumphs and instead of trying to overcome with violence, they transformed themselves and others by using peace.

Perhaps this is because the fighter uses violence to hide fear, or beat it down and conquer it. The peaceful person, on the other hand, defuses fear by identifying it and seeing that it is only something in your mind.

Let's look at Gandhi as an example. For years, Great Britain had ruled India as a colony. The Indian people wanted independence. Many people wanted a fight, wanted to take on the British army, which was one of the strongest in the world. Their leader, Gandhi, realized that the Indian people would never have the strength to beat the British and that thousands would die in a senseless fight.

Instead, he led boycotts, protests and hunger strikes to drive the British out. This was Gandhi's genius. He knew that eventually it wouldn't be worth Britain's time to stay in India, not if all the citizens were refusing to cooperate. In the end, Britain had no choice but to grant India's independence.

I know it may not seem cool or fun to be peaceful. Our society glamorizes the strong, the tough and the violent. But it is the one who walks away without using violence that is the real winner. You see fear and anger are powerful emotions that most people cannot control. A fit of anger is like a giant sneeze, and most people are unable to hold it back.

We are not victims of our emotions, or at least we shouldn't be. Master your fear and anger so you can react positively to a difficult situation. You will be more emotionally advanced than 99% of the population. To be clear—I'm not saying to keep bullying quiet. If you're being bullied, you must let an adult know and find a way to resolve your problem. Lying down and taking someone's abuse is no good. Stand up for someone being picked on, especially if that someone is you.

MoMENT oF CHALLENGE

Next time you feel anger, try one of these strategies instead of using violence:

- Count slowly to 10, breathing in and out as slowly as possible. Repeat 3 times.
- Exercise. Go for a run, drop and give yourself 20 pushups, go for a bike ride. Yeah fitness!
- Listen to some music that reflects your feelings. You know, the angry kind.
- Clean. I know, it sounds weird (and kind of like a chore), but many people find that when they're angry cleaning helps work off the burning emotions. At least at the end, you'll get something positive out of it!

So whether you're a quiet, passive person who rolls with everything, or you get in fights constantly, think about my journey. I went from a victim, to a powerful fighter, to a peaceful warrior. For a while, I was in love with the power that fighting gave me, but it turned out that the real power I had was the knowledge that I could defend myself. Now, I use peace, and a peaceful ending is the best of all.

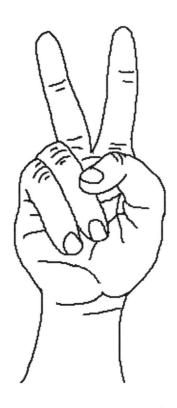

Life Lesson #10

The greatest fight of all is the fight inside of you. Listen to that voice inside of your head. Is that voice tearing you down or building you up? Make sure you turn the voice of pain into power by living in peace with yourself.

Discussion Questions

1) Explain how fear and fighting are connected.

2) What is the difference between fighting and bullying? How are they similar?

_____

_____

3) Is being passive a solution to bullying or violence? Why or why not?

_____

_____

4) Do you think the bully picks on others because they want to have fun or feel better about themselves?

_____

_____

5) Have you ever been a victim, bully, or bystander?

_____

_____

6) Agree or Disagree: "There are some problems that can only be solved with violence." Discuss

_____

_____

_____

_____

Chapter 11

Future

The Clock Is Ticking

"We all have our time machines, don't we? Those that take us back are memories . . . And those that carry us forward, are dreams."

–The Time Machine

Daydream of your life in five years, 10 years, or 25 years from now.

Hey! Did you just keep on reading without stopping?

I mean it. Do it. Daydream.

I know you get told all the time, "Think about your future! You've got to work to have a good future!" It gets old, right?

Well, I don't want you to think. I want you to dream.

You can start by imagining the surface stuff. How much money do you have in the future? Enough to get by, or piles of it? Are you driving a big car? Are you married? Do you own a home?

Now dig deeper. Imagine your daily life. Are you famous, or doing something behind the scenes to make the world better? Are you doing something to give back to the world? Are you working hard or are you living a life of leisure? Deep down inside, what are you doing that makes you happy?

There's no right answer for these questions other than YOUR answer. Not everyone dreams of being rich and famous. Many people dream of a quiet, successful career that allows them to help others and live contentedly. But unless you follow YOUR path to YOUR dreams, you'll live a life with a lot of dead ends.

Anyone can dream. It takes something else to live those dreams every day, knowing that your time and energy are going toward something you were meant to do. In this section, you'll see not just how to dream big, but how to live big.

Begin with the End in Mind

Did anyone ever tell you to always look one step ahead? But think about that saying. What would happen to you if you literally looked 12 inches ahead of your toes wherever you walked? I'll tell you, you'd be bumping into a lot of walls, stumbling into a lot of wrong bathrooms and you can forget about crossing the street safely!

No, you shouldn't look one step ahead. You should begin with the end in mind.

"Huh? But my future is so far away. Won't I get ahead of myself?"

You *should* live your life in each moment. Appreciate this moment because once it's gone, it's gone. But it's not impossible to live in the now and keep your sights set on the future. Most of us have goals and things we'd like to accomplish. Most of us are also aware that you have to work for what you want, unless you win the lottery. But the part people don't understand is that *you must plan backwards.* Think many steps ahead. Figure out what you want the big picture to look like; otherwise, you'll end up running into dead ends for a long time.

My own life is the perfect example of this. While I always knew I'd do big things, I never reflected on what I truly wanted in life. As a result, I spent many years chasing things I didn't really want.

Once I graduated high school, I was put in the position to think of what I wanted to become. So I had a lot of ideas in mind. I jumped from the idea of becoming a personal trainer, nurse, or radiologist. Then I said I wanted to become a doctor because my parents would be proud of me and I would make a lot of money.

Some people told me I should become a performer. Others said that I should be a CEO or TV host. I finally settled on becoming a dentist, and actually was a dental assistant for about two years to gain some experience within the field. Then I switched again and said, "You know what, maybe chiropractic school is right for me." I was interested in health and fitness and I thought chiropractic would be a great fit. So I got into massage therapy to learn about the human body and how it functions, and I thought I was set.

While I learned a lot from my experiences, I realized I wasn't feeling fulfilled in any of these jobs. I stopped to reflect on what made me happy, on what I really wanted for myself and how I wanted to help others. I knew I wanted to communicate and help people understand each other. I knew I wanted to work according to my own schedule and not for someone else's nine-to-five.

I knew I wanted to travel to awesome places and interact with people on a personal level. I knew I wanted a lot of money so I could support my family and give it back to the world that I believe is also my family. (Oprah and Michael Jackson, thanks for being that inspiration.)

That is what I really want in life, and that is what led me to become a speaker and coach, which led me to you! In fact, this is not the end of the road for me. I will continue to explore things that express my ultimate vision and highest excitement. I will always keep moving in a positive direction until I can reach as many people as I can! Whoa, I was in the moment!

Now look. I want you to try out new things. Jobs, hobbies, interests, friends, music, food, everything—go on, be daring, and see what you learn about yourself. But keep that "big picture" in sight. And that goal itself may change. Maybe when you get older you'll realize that what you wanted when you were 12, you don't want when you're 20. That's fine. What's important is to *have* a big vision to aim for and then take the necessary steps to transform that vision into your reality!

But getting back to my point, if you don't want to waste a lot of time, effort and money following paths that go nowhere, you need a big, long-term goal. Figure out what is most important to you.

Then, from there, think backwards.

If making a boatload of money is important, think about what career might lead you there. Then, think backwards from there. How hard is it to get into that job? What training do you need? What schools do you need degrees from? Then think backwards from there. How can you get into that school? What can you do NOW that will lead you to that FUTURE you imagine?

See, if I'd done that in my own life, I would've realized that personal training, nursing, radiology, dentistry and chiropractic work weren't right for me. But I didn't think "big picture" like that. I thought one step ahead.

Dreaming and Doing

So now, in your head, you're figuring out all the amazing things you want to do in life! You're thinking of big plans! In your future, you're living a fulfilling life with total happiness and satisfaction!

Dreaming big is one half of the equation for finding a successful future. The other half is doing big. Dreaming big will give you the vision, the focus and the drive. It will guide you towards what you want. But you have to get there somehow. That's the doing. You get to the doing by being real with yourself.

Sometimes, reaching our dreams means taking a series of small steps. Sometimes, it requires a giant, terrifying leap of faith. In either case, dreaming without action will ultimately lead to disappointment.

What action should you take? Well, what are your goals? For some people, it may mean leaving a career that is safe but unfulfilling to risk doing something new. It may mean connecting with people you don't know. It may mean moving, traveling or trying new things. It will almost certainly mean learning a lot.

I believe education is critical. I speak at schools and conferences all the time and I love working with students. However, I'm NOT going to tell you that school is the only place to get an education.

Shocker, right?

The best way to get an education is through life.

For many people, school is where they learn about life. Not just about math and literature, science and history—although those subjects deal with the nature of life— but about social interaction, working in groups, respecting others and ourselves and discovering our interests.

Take deadlines; if you take them seriously and learn to respect them in school, you'll learn to respect them when you work for a boss or when you have people working for you. Planning and organization are skills. If you're weak at them, improve them. Trust me, as life goes on, you'll need to be more organized and take on more responsibility than you do now. School can be like a giant sandbox of life where we can explore our interests without the obligations and responsibility that come with the "real world."

Going to school and hating it is the worst feeling. You have no energy or enthusiasm, and it drains all your creativity and inspiration. Instead of feeling like a victim, take control of your decision to go to school, great things will happen. Squeeze every drop of learning out of it that you can. Even if you hate class, hate homework and hate your teachers, I guarantee you can get something out of school. A friend, a lesson learned, a piece of wisdom.

Whatever your dreams require—years of schooling, competitive grades, and endless studying, or something you can achieve without a degree—don't make school a total waste of time. There are things to be learned there, inside the classroom and out.

So what does this all have to do with dreaming and doing? My point is that every little kid says, "I want to be this when I grow up," or "I want to do that!" That's the dreaming, imagining the most seemingly impossible things that can make you happy. The doing is taking those steps—the little tedious ones and the big scary ones—to reach that dream. If education is a necessary step, then do your very best so you can reach that dream. If education is not necessary, learn everything you can, because if you've got to be there, you may as well get something out of it.

Don't Pay for Today with Tomorrow's Credit Card

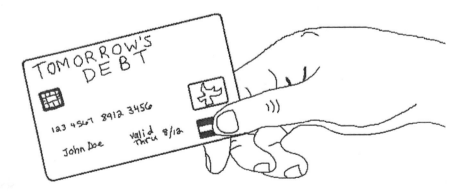

Pretty soon, you may have a job of some sort—maybe part-time at a restaurant or grocery store, maybe once in a while babysitting or mowing lawns. In either case, it's pretty sweet to have money in your pocket, isn't it? And I'll bet the money doesn't stay there long.

Bad news, friends. As you get older, things only get more expensive. Want a car? Expensive. Want a college education? More expensive! What about a house? Crazy expensive! The money for these things won't come magically, and you can't always count on credit. No, you need to save.

I know, saving money doesn't seem cool and definitely doesn't seem fun. But it's what separates the people who always seem to have money from the ones who never do. There are two keys to saving: do it a little at a time, and never, ever let yourself touch your savings except for its original purpose.

Let's say you babysit one night per week, and you get $25 each time. Each time you do it, instead of blowing all that money at once, stick five bucks (or even better, 10) in a separate envelope. You can label the envelope "Car" or "Trip to Europe" or just "Future." At the end of the year, you'll have more than $250 in it (or $500 if you saved more). You won't miss the little money taken out, and you'll have a big pile of it to put toward your future goal.

Even better is getting a savings account. Many banks have free savings accounts, and you'll even earn interest on the money there— the bank literally pays you to keep your money with them.

What happens to people who don't save? They work. And keep working. And keep working more, and wonder why they never seem to have any money. The people who save seem to have more money, even if they don't. They just make responsible choices so their dollars do more.

Money is like your energy and focus—if you don't make good choices about what you're doing with it, it won't do anything for you. Remember this in a couple chapters, when we talk about focus.

But Yahya, the Future is So Far Away!

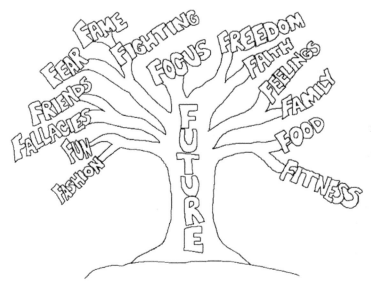

It's not, though. It starts a second from now. It starts in the next minute. Your future is like a tree whose seeds you're planting today, except if you ever decide you don't like the tree, you can plant new seeds and start over.

It happens in every generation. When you're young, the future seems far away, something you don't have to worry about until, well, the future. Then life happens. Suddenly, you're old, and you look back and wonder how life took you where it did, and how things could've been different.

I don't want that for you. I don't want you to be a passenger in your life. Remember:

Create your future! It's your life!

That's really the reason you should start caring right now about your future. The future can be anything you want it to be, but it's the only one you've got. Intentionally shape your future so it's uniquely yours. If you sit back and accept whatever comes your way, fine, but don't go whining later that life didn't turn out the way you wanted or expected. Whining and playing victim is playing weak.

Your dreams may seem ridiculous, absurd and unrealistic. Our present-day world is filled with drama, with bad economies, with a lot of unhappiness and fear. Maybe you've suffered through some pretty bad experiences, and you've made yourself believe that because of them, you'll never be able to achieve your dream.

Let me tell you about someone famous who achieved great things, even though life dealt him a pretty rough hand.

What are some things that all baseball players need to be great? A fast swing, great running speed a sharp eye, coordination and agility?

How about two hands?

Jim Abbott didn't even have that.

Born without a right hand, Abbott had a very good reason to never even try baseball. And all through his childhood and career, people added to that pressure, insisting that maybe he was talented for a handicapped player, but would never go far. Abbott never listened to that. He worked on his coordination by throwing a rubber ball against a brick wall, and developed a special technique where he would prop his glove on the stump of his right arm, pitch, then switch the glove onto his left hand. How did he do?

Jim Abbott was a star college pitcher, pitched for the 1988 U.S. Gold Medal Olympic Team and had a successful 10-year professional career, pitching for four different baseball teams. He even threw a no-hitter! He retired in 1999 and is an inspiration to many people.

There. Now put your obstacles in perspective. If Jim Abbott can achieve his dream, can't you find the same courage?

Besides that, there will be people all around you who will try to tear you down, who try to tell you that your dreams are just too far out of reach, so why not settle for something more reasonable. I say, DON'T settle for something reasonable. Dream big, then plan backwards and figure out how to reach that "impossible" dream. Plan 10 steps ahead but act one step at a time. If I want you to take one thing from this chapter, it's this:

Be daring in your dreaming and strategic in your doing.

MOMENT OF CHALLENGE

If you don't already know what your dream future is, take a few moments and reflect on what's important to you. I don't mean money or a specific job, but what values or principles matter most? What are your strengths? What are you really good at that not everyone can do? Then plan backwards and consider what careers might lead you to that. Maybe do a little research and find out what goes into starting that career.

Next, write that goal in big letters on a piece of paper and hang it somewhere you look at every day.

Finally, think of just one thing you can do today to start on that path. And do it.

> ## Life Lesson #11
>
> It's not just about the information you learn, it's also about the implementation. Our dreams become a reality once we take the necessary steps to follow through with our goals. Period.

Discussion Questions

1) What two things must you do to achieve your desired future?

   _____

   _____

2) What does it mean to "begin with the end in mind?"

   _____

   _____

3) What was Yahya's mistake in choosing a career?

   _____

   _____

   a. What did he learn from that mistake?

   _____

   _____

4) How do you feel about school?

   _____

   _____

   a. What do you, personally, get out of school?

   _____

   _____

5) Explain what Jim Abbott's story can teach us about reaching our dreams.

6) Agree or Disagree: "Some dreams are impossible to achieve." Discuss.

_____

_____

_____

_____

CHAPTER 12

Focus

The Key for Success

"One reason so few of us achieve what we truly want is that we never direct our focus; we never concentrate our power. Most people dabble their way through life, never deciding to master anything in particular."

—Tony Robbins

"**C**ome on, focus! Pay attention!"

"You have to focus if you want to succeed!"

"Hey! Focus, focus, focus! Work harder!"

"Your essay needs more focus."

You've probably heard teachers, parents or speakers say things like this before. Ever had it said to you? "Focus" is one of those catchwords that adults like to throw around, as if just it telling you to do it will make bad grades turn good, turn lazy students into Ivy Leaguers and transform sloppy work into a masterpiece. They'll say, "If you only had some focus, you could do anything," like it's some sort of magic power.

Well, it is!

I'm not talking about Harry-Potter-wizards-and-wands kind of magic, though. I'm talking about a skill that once you've mastered it, will enable you to do almost anything. People without it will look at you with awe because you'll be achieving things left and right while they stay stuck. With enough focus, you'll become a leader, a role model and maybe even a hero.

What's the catch?

It's harder now, more than ever, to focus. And every day our world makes it harder still.

But keep reading. The fact that you've stuck with this book so long is a great sign—it means you already know something about focusing! You must be one of the few, the proud, the focused.

Get ready to feel the magic.

Hey! Over Here!

According to Merriam-Webster Dictionary, "focus" has a number of meanings that are part of both science and everyday life. It means "to concentrate attention or effort" and "to adjust one's eye or a camera to a particular range." It also refers to "a point of convergence of a beam of particles." In every case, it basically means this: your focus is your point of concentration.

Science can give us a great illustration of the way focus works. Both light bulbs and lasers send out light energy. The light bulb sends it out all over the place, in different directions. The laser concentrates it all very tightly on one spot. Same type of energy, but that energy is so intense that the laser can cut through steel and burn holes in solid rock. Magic? No, but compared to the ordinary light bulb, it seems like it. A focused person is like a laser, using his or her energy to accomplish incredible tasks, while an unfocused person is like a light bulb—they might be doing a lot, but not really making much of an impact.

Fore!

Tony Robbins, who is one of the best peak performance coaches out there, and a person who has inspired me, has a lot to say about clarity and focus. "Clarity is power," he says, and "Whatever you focus on, you will find it.

We've talked about clarity before in the chapter about future. Clarity is your vision, your dream, your big goal. With clarity, you can visualize what you want and predict the challenges that will come your way. Without clarity, you'll be searching for your big goal—if you even know what it is—in the dark.

Focus is the other half of the equation for success. Clarity means nothing if you can't put your energy and attention towards that dream. Focus happens when you block out distractions and put all your attention on the one task in front of you. When your clear vision guides the intense force of your focus, almost anything can be accomplished.

Maybe you've never golfed before. Okay, probably not. But it does make a great analogy (I swear, your English teacher did NOT pay me to write this) for the way focus works. Imagine you're standing at the tee, preparing to take a shot. The hole is your dream, your goal of your eventual self. You look out over the course, noticing the rise or fall of the fairway, the trees and sand traps, the direction of the breeze. This is your clarity, scoping out what you eventually want.

But then, you have to shut everything else out as you look down at the ball on the tee. You can't think about what you'll be having for lunch, or about what your boyfriend/girlfriend said to you the day before, or about whether you're any good at golf, or anything like that. It has to be just you and the ball. The driver or club is your focus. When you swing it, your energy and attention will be in line with your goal, setting you up for success. Golf is a mental game, and so is life—if your head's not in it, the rest of you will be lost, too.

Perhaps you know someone who seems to do incredible things, and you want to know what the secret is. Maybe they always get excellent grades, or they're top athletes in your school, or they create amazing music or artworks. Sure, talent is some of it, but the real secret is this: Elite anyones—athletes, artists, students, you name it—agree that you perform best when you're "in the zone" and in order to succeed, you need to practice getting yourself there to perform your best.

Ooh! Pretty Colors!

So if one of the keys to greatness is so available, why isn't the world filled with super-achievers?

The same reason people don't get their homework done.

The same reason you meant to clean your bedroom, but time just got away from you.

The same reason some people might not have finished reading this book.

Distractions.

Anything can be a distraction. Siblings, Facebook, even a loud noise. What makes distractions so much sneakier nowadays is that they're so *tempting*. Today's distractions aren't annoying; they're calling to you. Just send a quick text. Just hop on Facebook. Just check what's on T.V. Send an email, or check to see if you have new ones. Wondering how your team is doing? A quick look online will answer that. Before you know it, minutes turn into hours that just slip away, which turns into days and years. There are a thousand distractions that nibble away at your time and energy, each one more tempting than the last. It's flat-out more difficult to focus now than it was 100, 50, even 20 years ago.

What do these distractions do? Think about light bulbs and lasers again. It spreads your attention and energy in a bunch of different directions so that you're always doing something, but seldom anything productive. Or using the golf analogy, you pay so much attention to the chirping birds, your ringing phone in your pocket or thoughts about breakfast that you can't clear your head and make a decent shot. Distractions are so powerful because we *let* them into our lives.

Some distractions only last a second, but others can grab your attention for years. Sometimes we chase things without thinking, letting them lead us to dead ends. If you don't keep your attention zeroed in on your goal—like a laser beam—you might find yourself looking back on the years, wondering what went wrong and why you never got what you wanted out of life. Yuck!

Ready . . . Aim . . . Succeed!

So we've talked about the importance of focus. Are you wondering how to improve your focus on your own goals?

I didn't think so. You're smart. You've figured it out already.

Get rid of distractions!

Before anything, you need a clear vision of your goal, as we discussed in the *Future* chapter. You need to know your steps to getting there, as well. So let's assume you're working on step one right now. You're getting ready to study, or plug in your guitar, or go for a run.

Then a thought tickles your brain.

You wonder if anyone's commented on the photos you posted.

You should check the score, just one last time.

Did she text you back yet?

What should you do?

Follow your dream!

Remember, distractions may tempt us to pay attention to them, but don't let them win! There are interruptions we can't do anything about, true, but there are plenty we can control. I guarantee, the more you ignore those little teases, the quieter they'll be. Pretty soon, you'll be free from the need to respond to them. Not that there's anything *wrong* with T.V. or phones or the online world. They can be awesome, but if you let them rule your life and take away from your real goals, you'll never reach where you want to be.

MoMENT oF CHALLENGE

Unplug for a night. For one night, don't go on the computer, don't text or check your phone, don't play your game system and don't watch any T.V. What can you do with your time? Whatever you want, as long as it isn't electronic. Read, clean, exercise, play a board game, talk with your family, go to sleep early. The choice is yours. I bet you can't do it for a full week. Go ahead. I DARE YOU.

I'll be honest (well, I'm always honest, but I'll be extra-honest here . . . wait, I just lied. I'm not *always* honest. Sometimes I lie. I guess that makes me honest for telling the truth. Interesting how that works, isn't it?). I should be the last person in the world to give advice on focus. I can be a scatterbrain. Ideas pop in and out of my head all the time. I have lots of energy and move from one thing to the next at lightning speed.

But my own struggles with focus have taught me a lot about it. In particular, one thing I've learned a lot about is multitasking. Some people are great at it. They can have a conversation with one person while texting another while thinking of what to have for dinner while doing their homework. I can't do that well. Really, *most* people can't do that well. In my experience, it's better to focus on doing one thing well before moving on to the next.

Your result will be so much better when you concentrate all your energy on one task. And really, that's what focus is. It's more than just doing well in school. It's about taking all your attention and concentrating it on one thing. Once you've learned to do that thing well, you can apply those skills to all areas of life. As the late Steve Jobs once said (you know, the main man behind Apple), "People think focus means saying yes to the thing you've got to focus on. But that's not what it means at all. It means saying NO to the hundred other good ideas that there are. You have to pick carefully."

It helps to have some more tricks in your bag. Here are some strategies that will help you improve your focus:

1) Eliminate your Distractions

We have so many distractions that grab our attention without our permission. Facebook, texting, phone calls, emails and random conversations that can be a waste of your time and energy are little things that get in the way of the big picture. Seriously, if there is a "top" tip that I would give anyone who is struggling with focus, it would be to eliminate the good and the bad distractions so you can focus on the great things that you can have, become and do.

2) Write your Goal Down

It's one thing to have a goal, but the simple act of writing it down will force you to remember it and think about it. It will also hold you accountable to the things you want to achieve. Studies have shown that people who write down goals are more likely to achieve them than people who don't.

3) Keep it Visible

Writing the goal down is great. What's even better is constantly reminding yourself of it. Make your goal into a poster and hang it in your room. Make it the background on your cell phone. Make sticky notes. *Seeing* your goal in front of you will help you literally keep it in your sights.

4) Silent Time

Meditation, prayer or even just quiet sitting can help improve concentration immensely. When you intentionally shut out all distractions and begin a practice that clears your mind, you'll find that your focus becomes much sharper. We live in a noisy world with lots of stimulating stuff—a little time away from that will help you keep things clear.

5) Throw Things OUT of Perspective

Huh?

If you look at things in perspective, the little distractions seem harmless. Surely, a quick text message or a half hour of T.V. isn't going to ruin your whole future. Thinking of it that way, it's easy to let distractions rule your life, one moment at a time. Instead, set up a ridiculous comparison. Give yourself only ONE choice. Would you rather:

- Update your status or become a professional musician?
- Send a text or become a vet?
- Watch another online video or become a graphic designer?
- Watch the rerun of that sitcom or own a business?

See, when you phrase it like that, it sets up your choices so the distractions seem much more powerful—and much less appealing—than they really are.

6) Start Small, Work your Way Up

It's very difficult to go from constantly distracted to uber-focused. Focusing is a skill, and like any skill, it improves over time. Next time you are working on a step toward your goal, set a time limit—say, for 10 minutes, ignore ALL distractions. Soon, you'll go for 20 minutes, a half hour, then an hour. Allow yourself to listen to the distractions, but later. Setting aside specific, small blocks of concentrated time will build your focusing skill.

We live in a busy world. It's a world with a thousand little electronic mosquitoes that nibble at us and suck all of the concentration out of us. Don't let them win. It's your choice to focus or not focus, and if you choose to indulge those pesky distractions, you may never reach that big goal. You're stronger than that. Shut your door, imagine your ideal future self, and take action. It really doesn't take any magic after all.

Life Lesson #12

"F.O.C.U.S.= **F**ollow **O**ne **C**ourse **U**ntil **S**uccessful"
-Social Media Expert, Mari Smith

Discussion Questions

1) **What do light bulbs and laser beams have in common? How are they different?**

   _____

   _____

   a. **Which one is the better example of what focus should be?**

   _____

   _____

2) **Explain why you need both clarity AND focus to accomplish a goal.**

3) **List three things that distract <u>you</u> from your goals.**

   a. **What can you do to eliminate the power of those distractions?**

   _____

   _____

4) **Explain how throwing things out of perspective works to improve focus.**

5) What would happen to you if you didn't use your phone or computer and just hung out with your family and friends?

_____

_____

6) Agree or disagree: Someone who is always busy must be very focused." Discuss.

_____

_____

_____

_____

CHAPTER 13

Fame

All Eyes on You

> "If you come to fame not understanding who you are,
> it will define who you are."
>
> —Oprah Winfrey

So maybe you've been dreaming of your future, and you've visualized what it's going to look like. You don't know all the details yet, or how you're going to get there, but you know one thing for sure:

You want to be *famous.*

I mean, wouldn't it be awesome to have an entourage or a bunch of fans and followers?

To give interviews and sign autographs?

To ride in limos, get free stuff and have your poster on kids' walls?

It doesn't seem to matter what you do or how you get there, but these days, getting famous is a goal all in itself.

My question is this: Why?

What is the *point* of being famous?

Fame is a strange creature. Some people work hard for years and years and never get well known. Other people do absolutely nothing and find themselves in the spotlight. Some people become famous through good deeds and inspirational acts, while others heap negative attention on themselves through doing things that are foolish, degrading or despicable.

Now, I'm not going to tell you *not* to become famous, either. You see fame, like so many things in life, isn't good or bad on its own. It all depends on what you do with it. You can become famous and use your fame to be a leader, an inspiration and a lighthouse to people who need guidance. Or you can become a disaster, an embarrassment, or 10-car pileup.

The choice is yours.

The Lighthouse

I'm sure you've seen a lighthouse, or at least a picture of one. The job of the lighthouse is to shine a bright light out into the ocean so that ship captains can see they are approaching land, and should use caution. Captains depend greatly on lighthouses, because if it's night or if there's a lot of fog on the water, it's very possible to crash into the rocks without even knowing they're there. The lighthouse uses its light to help others find safety and success.

The lighthouse is a metaphor (I know, I know! Again!) for the positive power of fame. If you gain lots of attention for what you do, that attention can be used to help make the world a better place. The lighthouse has light, but uses it to help others. With your life, you can shine brightly and inspire people, lift them up, teach them and be a positive example.

Let me give you two examples of "lighthouses" so you can see what I mean. The first is Will Smith. First off, Smith is just crazy talented. He started with a successful rap career, translated that into a T.V. career on *Fresh Prince of Bel-Air* and really burst onto the scene in films such as *Independence Day, Men in Black, I am Legend and now Men in Black III*. He's made millions upon millions of dollars, is one of Hollywood's biggest sure-things, is considered an A-list stars and has his children following his footsteps!

But what I admire about him is that through all of his fame and money, Smith has kept it real. He has a happy family and maintains privacy for them. He's physically very fit and his relationships are healthy. It looks like the man has it all figured out! How can he be a superstar celebrity, but still keep his life from spinning out of control, as it does for so many famous people?

The fact is, Will Smith is well grounded. He knows himself. He realizes that though he may be rich and famous, there's more to life than that. He keeps his life in perspective, and keeps his priorities straight, and this empowers him to be a movie star, a great husband, a loving father and a happy human being all at the same time.

A second person who has used fame to do good things in the world is Oprah Winfrey. You've probably heard of her; she's considered one of the most influential, important people today. Oprah is wealthy, powerful and famous many, many times over. Though she grew up so poor that she wore a sack for a dress until age six, and was a victim of sexual abuse until age 14, she has gone on to find incredible success and innumerable contributions to society:

- She is the first African-American woman to become a billionaire in American history.
- Her highly successful talk show *The Oprah Winfrey Show* ran for 24 years and won numerous Emmy awards.
- She has gained praise for her acting in films such as *The Color Purple* and *Native Son*.
- Her Book Club helps guide many people to become smarter, more sensitive readers and inspires thoughtful discussions of books. She is also an author of five books.
- She has donated millions of dollars to charities, and even founded the Oprah Winfrey Leadership Academy for Girls in Johannesburg, South Africa.

As you can see, Oprah gets lots of fame and attention. Along the way, she has spoken honestly and openly about her own struggles, fears and obstacles. Her genuine attitude makes people trust her, follow her and believe in her. Many people find her inspirational—I know I do. It's not just that she doesn't let fame lead her down a bad path; she actively *uses* her fame to get her message out and make the world better. Fame, for her, is a vehicle that carries hope to many people.

The 10-Car Pileup

Unfortunately, not all famous people are as admirable as Will Smith or Oprah Winfrey. Some of them find their lives ruined by fame. You've probably seen their pictures and stories all over tabloids in the supermarket checkout. It seems like every week they get into more and more trouble. Watching their lives is like watching a massive car wreck. It isn't pretty; you know on some level that what you're seeing is tragic and heartbreaking, but your eyes can't look away as the destruction gets worse, and worse, and worse. These people mistake all the attention and freebies as love, and then when they realize they don't have any healthy, loving relationships, they go off the deep end.

Look at someone like Lindsay Lohan. Talk about a walking car wreck! Her acting career began very young, and by the time she was a teenager she was being seen as a star for her roles in *The Parent Trap, Freaky Friday* and *Mean Girls.* She seemed poised for a great, successful acting career.

Then something went wrong.

In 2007, after her third car crash in two years, she was arrested for DUI. She went to rehab, but then was arrested for DUI and drugs again. In 2008, she was arrested for violating her probation. In 2011, she stole a $250,000 necklace and was sentenced to four months in prison. By her 25th birthday, she'd lived a life filled with more crime and mistakes than most people experience in their whole lives, and worse, she doesn't seem to be taking steps to make things better. That might all change in the future. Since she's still alive, she still has the power to take control of her life, if she wants to of course.

Another, even more tragic example is rocker Kurt Cobain. Cobain was the creative force behind the band Nirvana, whose music changed the 1990s. Their hit "Smells Like Teen Spirit" became an anthem for teens that were fed up with the world. Nirvana sold millions of albums; Cobain became a superstar and was already being called a musical revolutionary.

But while this was happening, his life was crumbling. His marriage to another rock star, Courtney Love, was unhappy and filled with fighting. Cobain was depressed and felt alone. The more famous the band became, the more he tried to hide, and he came to hate his fame. Then on April 5, 1994, he took his own life. The fame that he'd struggled so hard to earn ended up driving him to suicide.

Why Fame?

So with all these stories of people destroyed by fame, why do we want it so badly? Really, it comes down to our need for validation. Every person needs and wants validation; even the shyest, most modest person needs to be acknowledged once in a while. Some people need validation so badly—because of their personality, because of their childhood or for whatever reason—that they'll do anything to get in the spotlight, and anything to stay there. These people, who worship fame just for the sake of fame, often fall apart.

Also, don't forget one of the big sacrifices you must make as a famous person. One thing most teens want badly will be the first thing to be sacrificed because of your fame: privacy. Interviewers, tabloids, paparazzi and reporters may follow you around and snoop into stuff that isn't any of their—or anyone else's—business. But guess what? That's the price of fame.

And don't even get me started on issues of privacy! How annoying is it when your mom or dad goes into your room without telling you? Now imagine dozens of total strangers following you around, nosing into your business, not just asking you questions, but asking everyone you know: all your old friends, enemies, teachers and neighbors. I'm not trying to scare you out of seeking fame, but you should know the costs.

MoMENT oF CHALLENGE

Next time you feel like you want attention or want to be noticed, try to find a way to earn that attention through something positive. For example, in class, rather than making stupid noises or nasty comments, make an intelligent comment about the topic.

I understand the position of the attention-seeker and the class clown. I was one. From what you've read about my family life, it's pretty apparent I wasn't getting much positive attention at home. To meet that need for attention, I acted up a lot. I was your class clown type, and I'd say mean or rude things to get a laugh. Frankly, I was pretty obnoxious. Then one day my English teacher pulled me aside. She said she knew how smart I was and knew I was a good person. I was making some bad choices about what to do with my attention.

You see I have a knack for getting people to notice me. I'm good at grabbing hold of the crowd, but what my teacher showed me was that my ability could be used to lift the world up or drag it down. Up to that point, I'd been dragging it down. My teachers were frustrated with me, my classmates were annoyed and my GPA was a stinky 2.3 (that's around a C-). But my teacher told me that under all my shenanigans was a unique ability to inspire and lead.

Wow! Imagine how that changed my life right then. I realized I could fulfill my need to get attention and validation, but I could do it in way that could inspire and motivate a person, which is what I hope I can do for you, rather than make a fool of myself. The ability was there. The choice was mine.

You're in the same position, too. Whether you want to become a superstar or you like to stay behind the scenes and out of view, whether you're a class clown or the quietest kid in class, I urge you: don't waste your unique abilities on stupid stuff that gets you nowhere. Use your talents and personality to lift people up. You'll feel like a superstar on the inside, and that way, when fame comes to you, you'll stay steady. Don't be a car wreck; be a lighthouse. The lighthouse might not be as entertaining to watch, but it sure is the better one to be.

Life Lesson #13

Our deepest need is the need to be validated. Use your ability to get attention in a positive way and people will admire and respect you and the things you have done for years to come, even beyond your own life. Now, *that's deep.*

Discussion Questions

1) **What are the positive qualities of fame? What are the negative ones?**

   _____

   _____

2) **What separates people who use fame for good from those who let it destroy them?**

   _____

   _____

3) Think of a famous person you admire.

    a. Have they done anything positive and inspirational with their fame? If so, what?

_____

_____

    b. Have they done anything stupid, dangerous, wasteful, or cruel with their fame? If so, what?

_____

_____

4) If you had all the money in the world and you became famous, what would you do with it?

_____

_____

Tip: How you answer this question shows a lot about your character.

5) Agree or disagree: Famous people are real fake. Discuss.

_____

_____

_____

_____

CHAPTER 14

Freedom

Fly Like An Eagle

"Freedom makes a huge requirement of every human being.
With freedom comes great responsibility."

—Eleanor Roosevelt and Spiderman's uncle.

Freedom.

You want it.

Everyone wants it.

But what is it?

Freedom is one of our most basic human needs and desires. It is one of those things that everyone says he or she wants, but no one actually understands or agrees on what it means. If you Google freedom, you'll find that it's "the quality or state of being free" (duh!) including "the absence of necessity, coercion or constraint in choice or action." This is a start—it basically says you aren't forced to choose or do something particular. But when you ask individuals exactly what their ideas of freedom is; it depends mainly on who or what they want freedom from.

Freedom from a tyrant?

Freedom from an unfair government?

Freedom from slavery?

How about freedom from being "nobody?"

Or for that matter, how about freedom from fame?

Freedom from drug addiction?

Freedom from parents?

Freedom from ourselves?

This is just a short list of the oppressive forces that have trapped people over the ages. Some people search for freedom alone, while others band together, but each individual has his or her own private battle to be free from something. Once you understand exactly what your battle is you can more clearly see your ultimate goals.

What Freedom is NOT

Let's focus on the freedom that most teens are in search of: freedom from parental control.

I know a lot about this. It was my personal struggle growing up. My parents were very strict with me and didn't give me much chance to explore or fool around. It made me really angry and frustrated, especially seeing my friends were out having fun while I had to follow my parents' rules and curfews.

What happened?

When I got old enough, I went off the rails.

I did a lot of the stuff that kids do when they rebel: I went out to parties, fell in with the wrong friends, did stupid stuff with alcohol and got into trouble.

At first I thought it was great. Finally—this was what I had wanted! I could do anything and my parents couldn't stop me! NOW I had total freedom! I should've been overjoyed about it.

Except I wasn't.

On the outside I might've looked like I was having fun, but part of me knew this wasn't what I'd really wanted. You see, I'd wanted freedom from my parents, but at that age I didn't really understand what freedom meant or what responsibility came with it. I had thought that being able to do anything I wanted was freedom. A lot of teens think this—maybe you do, too.

Let me tell you from my experience—that's not freedom.

It may seem like fun at first, but total freedom brings on its own set of problems. Besides the health risks and dangers that go with risky behavior, the real problem is that you'll only become prisoner of something new—addictions, bad friends or poverty. You'll go from wanting to escape the grip of your parents to wanting to escape the destructive forces you've brought into your life.

What happened to my friends who got to do whatever they wanted? Honestly, most of them went nowhere in life. When you're a kid and you're allowed to do anything, you end up doing nothing. They were so busy being "free" that they didn't pay attention to creating a good future for themselves.

"Okay, Yahya," you're asking. "Then what should freedom look like?"

Real freedom has boundaries.

Your parents probably don't give you curfews because they hate you, and probably don't stop you from drinking and doing drugs because they want you to be miserable. It's because they understand something we all learn, as we grow older. If you cannot put limits to your freedom and control yourself with it, your "freedom" may end up taking over your life.

Freedom without boundaries isn't really freedom.

For example, one of my old friends whom I grew up with was allowed to do almost anything he wanted. His parents didn't care about a thing. Their philosophy was it's a free country, do whatever you want. And so he did whatever he wanted. I'll admit, I envied his life and wished his parents were my parents at times. He literally had the ideal teen lifestyle. He didn't worry about his grades, not because he wasn't smart but because no one really cared. He was invited to every party there was and would always ask me to join him. I felt so cool to be his friend.

Seriously, when we were hanging out we felt like we were on top of the world. If a fight were to break lose, he was always there fighting and sometimes I joined in. No one came near us. I felt safe around him, as free as ever. That is, until he got heavily involved with drugs and binge drinking. Now he's doing time in jail because of the choices he made. Even worse, his younger brother committed suicide at the age of 19. I really don't know why. Maybe it's because he didn't have a good role model in his life. What do you think?

The problem is, he didn't have any healthy boundaries. He confused freedom and having fun for irresponsibility and making dumb choices.

Chaos, confusion and abuse took over his life. The unlimited freedom he had ended up limiting his own life and future. In fact, the excess of freedom given to him early in life, has removed all freedom from his adult life.

It's the same for all of us. When the door is opened to unrestricted freedom, irresponsibility emerges. We fight and argue to be free from our parents and other people's control, only to have it replaced with the dumb decisions we make based on our own desires.

Now I am not saying every teen that wants freedom is going to make bad decisions, what I'm saying is that a few healthy boundaries can't hurt.

MOMENT OF CHALLENGE

Now that we've discussed freedom a little bit, think about what you're trying to be free from in your own life. In your goal—your dream life—what does freedom look like? What relationships or practices could you develop to help you achieve it?

What Freedom IS

"All right, Yahya," you're saying with a sigh. "Then you're saying I should just let my parents run my life and not say a thing about it, right? It's better for me to live like a slave to them because if I have fun even once, I might start partying like a rock star and end up lying in a gutter somewhere. Is that what you're saying?"

Not at all.

Like I said in the beginning, freedom is one of our basic needs and desires. I'm only saying that total, unrestricted freedom could end up hurting you. However, you can—and should—seek more freedom in your own life. This means several different things:

1) Practice Open Communication and Respect

For some parents, giving up control is very difficult. They have watched you go from a helpless infant who constantly needed them to—in the blink of an eye—a confusing teenager with new interests, thoughts and desires. They believe that letting you run your own life means letting you ruin your own life. And they're not 100% wrong, either. After all, they do have years of experience on you.

However, in the end, it IS your own life, and they will come to see that, sooner or later. If both you AND your parents develop healthy communication and respect the transition to your independence will be smoother.

So how does that transition start?

You have to make the first move.

Be the first to open up. Be the first to show respect. This will make parents MUCH more likely to consider granting you independence.

Think of it this way—if you're in your own little world, and they are in theirs, you might feel as if you are free from them. But when you open up to each other's worlds, well, that's twice as much world! A mutually respectful relationship with parents can give you lots of freedom.

2) Know Yourself.

Duh. That's easy—everyone knows him or herself.

Not really. As I've mentioned before, many people go through life without truly understanding themselves, their desires or their tendencies. When you have a clear vision of these things for yourself, you are less likely to be sidetracked by temptations and distractions in the world.

3) Get Help

Some types of freedom simply cannot be won alone. If you suffer from the prison of alcohol or drugs, or are suffering abuse, you may not have the skills to become free all by yourself. By developing healthy relationships and looking within yourself, you can build a strong emotional foundation for your own freedom. But you just might need a trusted professional to get you there.

4) You're Already Free.

What?

Are you kidding me?

I really don't FEEL free.

And if this is true, why didn't you just say so at the beginning?

When you think about it, we already have the freedom to do literally anything we want. If I want, I could stop writing right now, get in my car, rob a bank, spend all the money on drugs, then fly to South America and live in the jungle. I could beat up anyone in my way, burn down a school, kick puppies and mug little old ladies. I have that freedom.

But I don't want that. Neither do you. (I hope!)

I also have the freedom to take every penny I earn, donate it to charity, then go to work helping people, who are in need, for the rest of my life.

You have that freedom, too.

I have the freedom to go out into the world and pursue my dreams. I also have the freedom to sit on my you-know-what all day and watch the world go by.

You have that freedom, as well.

And this gets to the very heart of what I hope you learn from my time with you and from this book: You have the freedom to make any choice you want, or do anything you want, for better or for worse. But with that freedom comes responsibility—you must accept the consequences of anything you do. You can control the choices you make but you CAN'T control the consequences. This is your life and future—now go make it look however you want it to look. You have that freedom and that power already. Practice the things we've talked about so far.

It won't always come easily. And it ALWAYS comes with responsibility, because you have to take ownership of every choice you make. Once you do that, you'll understand true freedom.

Life Lesson # 14

When you are true to yourself and realize that your freedom doesn't need to rely on changing others around you or on the material things of life (a new game, a boyfriend or girlfriend, a better family, a better car, a better career, a better hairstyle), then you have reached ultimate liberation. Freedom is hidden deep inside of you and you are the only person that can find it.

Discussion Questions

1) **What are some of the things people wish to be free from?**

   _____

   _____

   a. **What do they have in common?**

   _____

   _____

2) **What did Yahya originally think "freedom" meant?**

   _____

   _____

   a. **What happened to him when he achieved it?**

   _____

   _____

   b. **What did Yahya learn that real freedom has?**

   _____

   _____

3) **Explain what happens when someone gets too much freedom.**

4) **What are some things you can do to gain more freedom?**

_____

_____

5) **Agree or disagree: "We are already free." Discuss.**

_____

_____

_____

_____

CHAPTER 15
Faith

It's in Your Heart

"Faith is a knowledge within the heart, beyond the reach of proof."

−Kahlil Gibran

This short chapter is about faith. It is not about religion, nor is it about right vs. wrong or about me telling you "The Way." This chapter is about faith.

It is about peace.

It is about the one thing that all human beings, regardless of nationality, race, gender, religion, politics, sexual orientation or favorite sports teams share: our humanity.

I grew up in a diverse neighborhood. There were Blacks, Whites, Hispanics, Asians, Christians, Muslims, Hindus and Atheists, and I learned a little something from every background in my youth. And what I learned was this: People focus on their differences way too much. We may not have the same skin color or religious beliefs, but what we do have is shared emotional experience. People from every culture can laugh, cry and love. We all want to be free. We all want to be treated with respect.

Why spend all our time trying to scramble to the top and put others down? Doesn't it make more sense to tap into that common experience?

Freedom = Peace

When each individual realizes that we all have the power to determine our own futures, when each person treats every other person with fundamental respect, when everyone uses his or her power of choice to lift the world up and make it a better place, do you know what would happen? Do you know what that would create?

World peace.

Last chapter, we talked about how too much freedom without boundaries just creates violence and unhappiness. But real freedom can bring peace. When we understand that we are not victims in our lives (unless we CHOOSE to be) and that we are all in search of something in life, there will be no more need for violence or struggle.

What does this have to do with faith?

The word "faith" has, unfortunately, acquired a lot of baggage. For some, it means a guiding light through life. For some, it is a sword used to hack down people who don't agree with you. And for others, it's a fortress they hide behind to avoid the risk of being wrong. Some people think faith is a beautiful thing, while others find it offensive, and some just don't really care one way or the other.

So once again, let me repeat—we're not talking about religion.

If your faith is religious and it keeps you focused and strong, then great! Religious faith can be a very powerful personal guide for shaping your future.

Just remember, faith is a personal guide. For some people, it's like a guiding light. And others might have a different guide and that's okay.

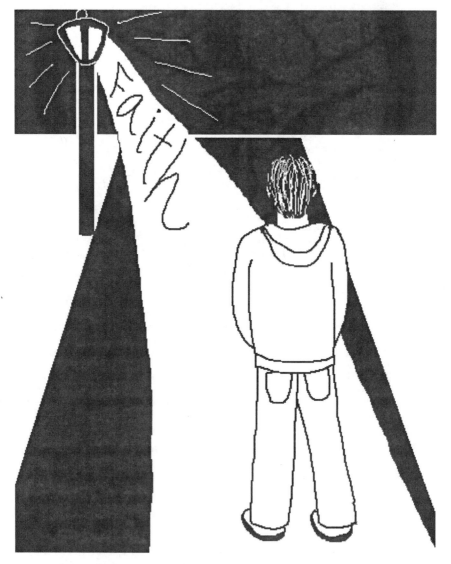

Trying to force your faith on others just doesn't make sense. Faith comes from within, so pushing it on others won't really make an impact, other than to irritate the other person. You're better off celebrating your faith—or your different faiths—than trying to make someone agree with you.

Many people, on the other hand, have no faith. Either they mock it or just ignore it, but figure that faith is just not part of their lives.

Well guess what? It's possible to have faith that isn't part of religion.

You can have faith in humanity. You can have faith in peace. You can have faith in love. You can have faith in yourself.

Whaaaaaat?

Look, faith just means that you believe in something without needing to have it scientifically proven. So, if you believe that all humans are essentially good—even though you know they sometimes do bad things—you have faith in humanity. Your belief in the goodness of mankind is *stronger* than the need for it to be proven to you.

MoMENT oF CHALLENGE

Do you have faith? If it is a religious faith, how do you use it to make the world better? If it is a non-religious faith, what is it you believe in, and how is it helping the world? Can you go out today and do one thing—using your faith—to improve our world without criticizing or judging others?

So let's sum up:

- Everyone wants freedom
- Everyone is already free—free to make choices and improve or hurt the world.
- Faith—of any kind—can be a guide to making our lives and the world a better place.
- We *always* have the freedom to accept or reject, to do good or do evil, to love or to hate, based on our faith.
- IF (and that's a big "if") everyone made choices that helped them achieve their own dreams, while at the same time respecting and supporting everyone else's efforts to do the same, the world would become peaceful.

We've come a long way together. We started out talking about keeping fun in your life, making good food choices and staying fit. Now we're ending with universal freedom and world peace. But it's all tied together. I've said it over and over and over:

Create Your Ultimate Life!

But don't forget—everyone you know has his or her own life to create, too. We're all on our own journeys, but we're not alone. We have friends and family to support us, and we have all of humanity to share our experiences with. In today's world, sometimes we're told that we have to claw our way to the top, be the best and crush the competition. But you know what? Real winners—the ones who truly reach their dreams, find happiness and peace and make the world better—don't have to climb their way to the top on the backs of others. Real winners get to the top by raising the whole world around them.

So now it's on you—go out there. Dream big. Do big. Climb on that bike and know your destination. Put premium fuel in your gas tank. Express yourself. Surround yourself with loving, supportive, positive people. Use your freedom of choice to make the world better. Keep your mind open and sharp. Love, laugh, cry, be healthy.

It's your life—now go and live it!

Life Lesson #15

All violence, hate and discrimination in the world can be put to an end once we understand who we really are and what we're capable of as humans. We might be different on the outside, but we are all the same on the inside. We all have blood, we all have a heart (you're alive and reading this book, aren't you?), we all have a voice, we all make mistakes and we all feel alone at one point or another. I encourage you to love more and judge less. When we judge others, we lose our ability to inspire or influence them in a positive direction. You can make a difference just by being you. Remember: Inner Faith Always Inspires Total Humility, Honesty and Humanity. (Inner F.A.I.T.H.H.H.) From my experience, that's one of the best ways to create an amazing life.

Discussion Questions

1) Does "faith" always mean "religion?" Why or why not?

_____

_____

2) Define "faith":

3) Do you have faith? If so, describe what you have faith in.

4) Explain how faith can bring peace to your life.

5) Agree or disagree: "In order to succeed, you may have to knock some people down." Discuss.

_____

_____

_____

_____

BONUS CHAPTER
Forgiveness

> *"The practice of forgiveness is our most important contribution to the healing of the world."*
>
> —Marianne Williamson

This bonus chapter doesn't need much explanation. It's pretty simple and that's why it's short and to the point.

You see, there will come a point in your life when someone, something or some event might hurt you so bad, that all you'll want to do in that moment is get back, get even and *take* whatever you can from them.

I can promise you this, it's not about how much you can *take*; it's about how much you can give.

Forgive them.

That's why I forgave the guy who punched me in the street for no reason. That's why I forgave my mother for leaving me when I was a baby. That's why I forgave my father for abusing me when I was growing up.

If you want real power, learn to forgive.

Now, I know you're probably thinking, "Well that's great Yahya, very motivational and all, but c'mon. Let's be realistic, it's easier said than done."

You're right . . . it *IS* easier to place the blame than take control of our problems, *BUT* it's still possible.

And here's the thing, I don't have to walk a mile in your shoes to know that you've been through some difficult times. From the day that you were born to this very moment, you might:

- Have been hurt through a tough break-up
- Have lost friends and family
- Have been abused or raped
- Have a disability
- Have been bullied
- Be using drugs, food and alcohol to mask your pain
- Be hurt so deep inside that you're thinking or have thought about taking your life away.

Look, I'm not going to try and act like I can relate to *ALL* of your experiences because the truth is, I can't. But I'll tell you what; you can use that source of pain, use that source of hate and frustration to bring out the worst in you or the best in you.

It's a choice.

If you look, there's proof all around us. My friend, Josh Shipp, was an orphan who was raped and abused. He tried to commit suicide 10 times. Can you believe that? Josh also had a choice. What did he choose? He decided to stop complaining about his past and start creating his future. Now he's a millionaire who inspires people to turn a mess into a message.

This is nothing new. We've all heard of people who've decided to take ownership of their lives by seeing the best in themselves. I call these people *leaders* and by leaders I mean *YOU*. You have the gift to lead your life in whatever direction you choose

I guess what I am saying is that in the end, we all have stories, but if you don't like your story, rewrite it.

We all have our problems, but if you don't like your problems, then change them.

Bottom line: take control of your life.

If you are blaming yourself or others, STOP. Blaming gets us nowhere; it keeps us stuck, wasted and feeling defeated. And we've all been stuck before, so don't use that as your excuse to not get that healthy body that you want, to not ask that girl or guy out, to not do your best in school and to not follow your dreams.

This is your life. Your future. Create it.

BONUS LESSON

It takes a bigger and stronger person to be more loving than more right. Forgive, let live and lead with your heart.

YOUR ULTIMATE CHALLENGE

Forgive someone who has hurt you. Forgive them today. Call, text, write or email them and express your feelings. Let the pain out and allow the love, happiness and joy to come back in. Allow the REAL YOU to come back to life. Don't worry about how dumb, stupid, or idiotic you might look, sound or feel. Just do it. You got this. I believe in you.

Acknowledgments

This book wouldn't have been possible if it wasn't for all the people who have challenged as well as inspired me to be who I am today. I have met a lot of people throughout my life and everyone is unique and valuable in their own way. Please forgive me if I don't remember your name. I might have forgotten in this moment but not forever. I still love and appreciate you for being a part of my life.

The Word is My Family

My biological mother: If it wasn't for you, I wouldn't have been here and that's a fact. I really hope I get to meet you one day. If not, I want you to know that I unconditionally love and forgive you.

My father: We've had our ups & downs but we've also come a very long way. You will always have a place in my heart and I love you for the human being that you are and the wonderful father you've become.

My stepmother: You are such a wonderful soul. You have raised me as your own since I was 5. I am grateful to have someone like you in my life and to be able to call you mom. I love you and I'm always here for you.

My stepfather: You have a great heart. Thank you for loving the way that you love. Ali is very lucky to have a father like you and so am I and so is Faris.

My brothers & sisters: You have all taught me so much. You're the main reason why I wrote this book. I am honored to be your older brother. I hope I am as much of an inspiration to you as you are to me. I love you so much Faris, Rania, Ali, Joey, Stef, Reema, & Mohammed.

My cousins, uncles and aunts: It would take me another book to write down all your names. You know who you are. I send my love to each and every one of you in Arizona, Jordan, Syria, Saudi Arabia, Egypt, Malaysia and Thailand. Thank you for being a part of my life. I love you!

My beloved Kate: Our relationship is a book on its own. You have seen me at my worst and my best. I have never met a person with your level of tolerance and ability to love unconditionally. I am so grateful to share my life with you. I couldn't ask for a better best friend. "I will always love you."

My extended family: The Fabers and Damianos. Thank you for allowing me to be a part of your life. I am appreciative for all the love and patience you have for me. Without you, none of this would have been possible. Especially Garry and Kathy Faber. I love you all.

My brothers from other mothers: Osama Janakat, Abe Sharkas, Antwan L. Penn, Mike Rubera, Kenny Beltran, Jorge Mantilla, Alit & Jetmir Vojka, Ervin & Mickey. You have been there for me through thick and thin. If I died tomorrow, I would die a happy man knowing that I had the opportunity to meet such amazing individuals in this life. I love you guys so much. "We're just a reflection of each other."

My Family Chiropractic and Wellness Center Buddies: Dr. Kevin Merlino, Kelly "bellies", Dariusz, Tasha, Dr. Andrea G. and all the patients who feel so much better after they visit. You have put up with my big mouth for far too long. Thank you for being my creative geniuses throughout this time-consuming process. You are all my family. I love you.

My "older" brother: Henry Yu, thanks for taking care of me. I am always here for you. You are a mentor, a friend but most importantly an older brother I never had. I send my love to you and the family.—Mini Yu

Fairfield family: Aaron, Tiamat, Janet, Theresa, Cookie, Jess, Yancy, Sam, Heyword, Puki, Krystal, Brandon, Schuyler, Nelson, Trina, Emily, Lauren, Guji, Carly, Frank, Sudiksha, Naresh, Arun, Justin, Leora, Professor Lerom, Brian, Stephen, Sean and more . . . AHHH!!! So many wonderful memories. I miss you all so much. I haven't forgotten you. You know who you are. I love you. "I still got my card ;)"

My Mentors: Brendon Burchard, Tony Robbins, Oprah, Stephen Covey, Neale Donald Walsch, Dr. Wayne Dyer, Deepak Chopra, John C. Maxwell, Dr. Joel Haber, Curtis Rasmussen, Henry Yu, Josh Shipp, Brooks Gibbs, Rich German, Joe DiRaffaele, Ty, Carol Hinson and my future mentors. I would literally be lost with out you. Thank you for your wisdom, spirit and belief in me.

My Team of Creative Geniuses

You have all went out of your way to help me out. Thank you for believing in me and being part of my journey. I love you all.

Book Illustrations: Lauren Tirpak, your artwork is indescribable. I see you doing amazing things. You are a gold mine of talent. Keep following your passion. I know your family is so proud of you, as am I.

Book Cover: EJ Negre, how many revisions did we have to go through? lol. Thank you for your patience and skills. I am so happy with the final product. I hope you get to meet Kanye West some day. Your work rocks!

Copywriting: Adam Knight, you are a lifesaver. Without you this book would literally be non-existent. Thank you for your time, hard work and faith. I appreciate you beyond words.

Editing: Kelly Faber, Stephen Saulpaugh, Elisha Griffis, Brandy Hadden, & Margaret Smith. Thank you for all the time and work that you've put into this book. I can't thank you enough. Kelly, thank you for helping me out in the last minute. I believe I was the cause of your migraines. No hard feelings. You're the best sister-in-lawyer :)

Web design: Brad, Barry, Grant, Kishan, and Chirag, words can't express what you've all done for me. I appreciate you guys so much. I can only hope there is a way I can return the contribution. I love you all!

Videography: Ramazan, Frank & John. WOW! You guys are going to make it big pretty soon. I'm watching you! Thank you for all your help. Thank you for believing in me. I'm so proud of us. "We are in this together."

Graphic Design and Photography: Angel, Keith, Harrison and Zoraida, you all have went out of your way to help me be where I am today, and for that I love you. I hope I am there for you in the same way you were there for me.

My colleagues: Josh Shipp, Brooks Gibbs, Fabian Ramirez, David Garcia, Jason Marshall, Dr. Joe Martin, Laymon Hicks, Blake Fly, Kantis Simmons, Sherita Titus, Hoan Do, Angel Matney, Annette Varoli, E Dub, Romeo Marquez Jr., Ryan Porter, Grant Baldwin, Michael Costigan, Tom Thelen, Mike Hall, Nick Palkowski, Clint Pardoe, Mark Black and the rest of the Youth Speaker University family, thank you for being a part of this journey. We are lifting up the youth together and I am honored to call each and every one of you my colleagues and friends:) I love you all.

Epic Coach Academy

The coach's coach: Rich German, you are one amazing individual. We both have great opportunities coming our way. Thank you for being a mentor and a great friend. Looking forward to go paddle boarding with you and the dolphins! I love you.

The coaches: We are a family now. We've shared our vulnerabilities and our successes with one another. I acknowledge all of you for stepping outside your comfort zone. Thank you for being a great example for me to follow. I love you.

Final Acknowledgment

To all my friends, fans and followers, you must know that I care so much about you. Please remember to always be true to yourself, love openly and forgive quickly. Words are too limited to express my gratitude, compassion and honor for being a part of your life and so I leave you with this:

From my heart to yours,
Much love and peace.

-Yahya

About the Author

The oldest of seven siblings, **Yahya Bakkar** is recognized as one of America's youngest leading authorities on the topics of life choices, bullying prevention and student leadership. He is a respected author and a highly sought–after youth speaker. Yahya is also a former 2-time National Jr. Olympic champion in Taekwondo and has trained with the top experts in personal development, human dynamics and teen behavior.

Like many people, Yahya faced many challenges growing up.

Born in Makkah, Saudi Arabia, he first traveled alone to the United States at the age of 5.

Abandoned by his biological mother, abused by his emotionally distant father, and mugged in the street at the age of 11, Yahya knows what it feels like to be "dealt the wrong hand."

By overcoming his challenges and continuing to learn from the universal school called "life," Yahya has made it his personal goal to empower teenagers and those who care about them to become caring and confident leaders.

His fans say, "He's awesome." His friends say, "He's larger than life." His family says, "He's a great role model." Strangers say, "He's like the energizer bunny." Yahya says, "In the end, I'm just one guy who would like to help our future generations help themselves."

To learn more, visit:
www.YahyaBakkar.com
www.NationalYouthSpeaker.com

To become a fan, visit:
www.YoYahya.com

CPSIA information can be obtained at www.ICGtesting.com
Printed in the USA
LVOW071616071212

310621LV00019B/939/P